# Babies
# Remember
# Birth

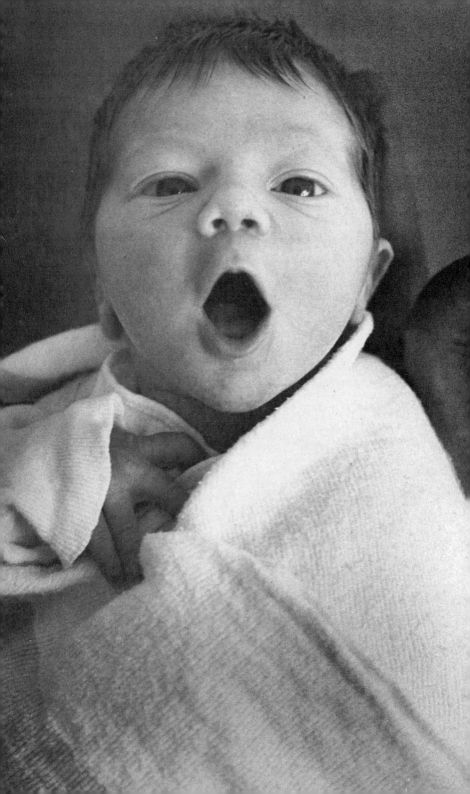

# Babies Remember Birth

*And Other Extraordinary
Scientific Discoveries about
the Mind and Personality
of Your Newborn*

David B. Chamberlain, Ph.D.

Ballantine Books • New York

Library of Congress Catalog Card Number: 89-90936

ISBN: 0-345-36411-2

This edition published by arrangement with Jeremy P. Tarcher, Inc., Los Angeles

Cover design by James R. Harris
Cover photo by George Kerrigan

Manufactured in the United States of America
First Ballantine Books Edition: January 1990
10  9  8  7  6  5  4  3  2  1

To
Donna Snouffer Chamberlain
midwife to
*Babies Remember Birth*

# CONTENTS

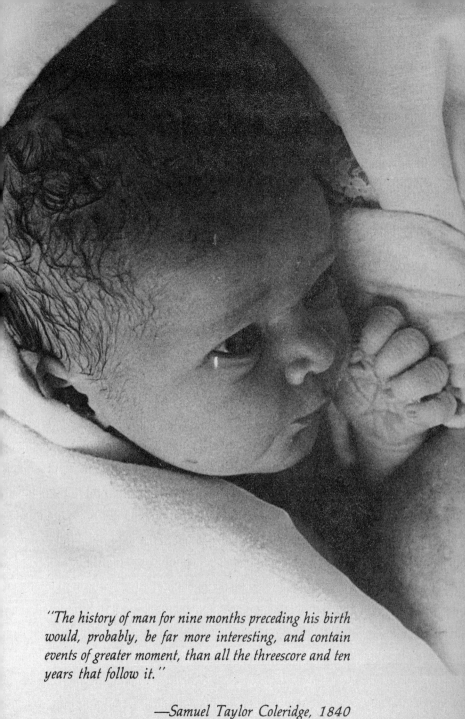

"The history of man for nine months preceding his birth
would, probably, be far more interesting, and contain
events of greater moment, than all the threescore and ten
years that follow it."

—Samuel Taylor Coleridge, 1840

# The Truth about Newborns

What do you see when you look at a newborn baby, bright-eyed, gazing straight at you? Is there really a person there? Silently frowning or beet-red with rage, can this baby think and feel? For its small size, a newborn makes a powerful, compelling noise, but is it actually *saying* anything?

Until recently, there were many theories about newborns but few known facts. For uncounted centuries, infants have been separated from the rest of us by a veil of ignorance. As close as we have been to them, we did not know how amazing they are. Common wisdom about babies was based on the obvious limitations of their size, weight, and muscle power.

Consequently, babies were described as sometimes adorable but incapable, subhuman, prehuman, dull, and senseless, and treated as such. Twentieth-century science has held that infant cries were only "random" sounds, their smiles only "gas," and their expressions of pain simply "reflexes." Misinformation about the newborn has made parenthood more difficult and infancy more miserable.

A brighter future has been dawning for infants. In the last twenty-five years, research on the newborn has flourished. An unprecedented combination of interest in infants, investment of large sums of public and private money, and innovative methods of study has resulted in new information, much of it surprising. Contributions to our widening knowledge of the newborn come from diverse fields of science, from embryology to psychology.

Because most of this information has been written in the language of specialists and found mainly in academic libraries, few parents have had ready access to it, or the time and opportunity to view these separate findings as a whole. This book gathers the most important facts from this wide literature for a general audience, especially new or prospective parents. While it is not a book footnoted for scholars, the interested reader will find sources and readings appropriate to each chapter beginning on page 203.

Leading researchers now sing the praises of infants. Harvard's Berry Brazelton calls them "talented"; Hanus Papousek, a German pioneer in infant studies, calls them "precocious"; famed pediatrician Marshall Klaus calls them "amazing." Edinburgh's Tom Bower, one of the most productive of all infant researchers, declares that newborns are "extremely competent" in perception, learning, and communication.

Babes have come of age in our century. Because so much has been discovered and momentum is still building, I think this will prove to be the century of the newborn, the time when we finally reach a full and factual knowledge of who they are.

At the beginning of this century, only a handful of scientific papers about infants could be counted worldwide. By midcentury, almost five hundred could be cited. In the 1960s and 1970s, serious reviews of this literature suddenly had to cover at least two thousand books and papers. This information explosion continues. Infants have been measured inside and out, filmed with cameras permitting analysis down to microseconds, watched for hours on end, and tested in clever experiments. Results show that they pick up information constantly and learn from their experience much as we do.

One of the exciting aspects of this new knowledge is the verification of infant abilities at earlier and earlier ages.

Timetables estimating the ages at which particular talents are expected to appear have had to be revised again and again, bringing them closer to birth. Many abilities are innate and adult-like, surprising investigators and ruining theories. A fundamental rule of developmental psychology —that all complex behaviors must start as simple behaviors and develop gradually—has become obsolete. Surprisingly, many behaviors *start out* complex.

The truth is, much of what we have traditionally believed about babies is false. We have misunderstood and underestimated their abilities. They are not simple beings but complex and ageless—small creatures with unexpectedly large thoughts.

Babies know more than they had been supposed to know. Minutes after birth, a baby can pick out its mother's face— which it has never seen—from a gallery of photos. Babies recognize the gender of other babies, even when crossdressed, provided they are moving—something adults cannot do. They are mentally curious and eager to learn. Consider how smoothly the senses are coordinated at birth: eyes turn with the head in the direction of a sound; hands go up to protect eyes from bright light; the first time at the breast, the baby knows how to suckle and breathe in perfect synchrony.

The territory of life *before* birth has also been charted as never before. Through the wizardry of the scanning electron microscope, fiber optics and special lenses, ultrasound imaging, and other measuring devices and laboratory techniques, we now have a comprehensive picture of development of all parts of the physical system before birth. These discoveries have added to our understanding of the baby's many talents.

Neuroscientists have discovered the timetable for development of the entire nervous system. For example, studies show that the sense of taste begins functioning around fourteen weeks after conception, and the sense of hearing around twenty weeks. After only eight weeks of gestation,

xiv ⋅§ BABIES REMEMBER BIRTH

stroking the baby's cheeks with a fine hair produces consistent reactions indicating that tactile sensitivity has already been established. During gestation, all the structures are set in place that will enable the newborn to use the sense of smell as well as any adult. Similar preparations are made for use of a wide range of visual talents. *Learning* before birth has even been demonstrated in formal experiments.

A host of scientific discoveries provides formal verification of what many parents and grandparents have known all along: newborns are real persons. Parental enthusiasm about newborn abilities used to be dismissed as vanity, bias, or hallucination. Now science confirms that infants are social beings who can form close relationships, express themselves forcefully, exhibit preferences, and begin influencing people from the start. They are capable of integrating complex information from many sources and, with a little help from their friends, begin regulating themselves and their environment.

## Myths about Newborns

**Babies Don't Feel.** Some nurses and doctors are still telling parents that babies don't really feel things—that they will not suffer during medical procedures, or miss their mothers if taken away to a nursery. Anesthetics have not been considered necessary for infants undergoing surgery. Hospital delivery rooms, obstetrical instruments, and medical routines were all designed before babies were thought to have senses and thus with no regard for babies' comfort. Rooms are frigid, lights blinding, surfaces hard and flat, the atmosphere noisy, the handling of newborns too upsetting. Newborns are routinely traumatized and punctured.

Generation after generation, an unlucky portion of male babies have been subjected to circumcision for supposed "medical" reasons (now denied), "religious," "cultural," or cosmetic reasons. I can only assume that parents have tolerated this in the mistaken belief that the baby will not know he is being tortured. He will.

Babies considered unable to feel are easily victimized; they become nonpersons with minimal rights. An earlier, more deadly, form of this view provided justification for infanticide (mostly female), practiced widely through most of human history. In modern times child abuse, the once secret violence of parents, is exposed to public view. Infants may be the last large category of persons to be fundamentally misunderstood, discriminated against, and abused.

In 1975 French obstetrician Frederick Leboyer called for a new approach to birth without violence. His colleagues denied the need for change and publicly recited the myth that babies do not really feel or care. The newly discovered truth is that newborn babies have all their senses and make use of them just as the rest of us do. Their cries of pain are authentic. Babies are not unfeeling; it is *we* who have been unfeeling.

**Very Poor Brains.** Probably the most damaging myths about newborns are those about their brains. Reasoning from the gross anatomy of the brain at birth, scientists concluded that it was "primitive" and poorly developed. And, because it was only about one-quarter of its eventual weight and volume, it was incapable of "higher" functions of thinking, meaning, and memory.

For a hundred years this assumption has governed both medicine and psychology, supporting abuses in obstetrics and pediatrics that are accepted as a normal part of birth. Without a brain, babies could have no experiences, accumulate no history, possess no self-consciousness or intelligence —in effect, could not really *be present.* This myth has artificially delayed the beginning of active parenthood and prevented public recognition that newborns are persons. The reasoning is this: no brain, no person; no person, no need for parenting.

In retrospect, brain experts made one of the classical errors of science by dissecting the brain to find out how it works. The problem is that the brain works properly only if it is whole. Separate parts are not the system. Most serious was the error of severing the brain from its connections with two other systems, the endocrine and immune systems. Medicine officially divided the territory into three different specialties: neuroscience, endocrinology, and immunology. Current research shows all three are elegantly linked in one fluid central intelligence system.

That the whole brain is more than its parts is illustrated by a debate that has lasted for decades over the myelin sheathing that insulates nerve fibers. I ran into this wall personally when I started to tell colleagues about the birth memories my clients were reporting. Their immediate reaction was that such memories were impossible because the myelination of nerve tracks was not complete at birth and therefore signals could not flow properly through the nervous system. The truth is that myelination begins in some places only a few weeks after conception but is not completed until adolescence. It is no measure of what a baby's brain can do.

**Assembly-Line Brain.**    Another basic misunderstanding about the infant brain was that it was like an engine on an assembly line, not expected to work until the last part was installed. Compounding this error was a prejudice that the parts of the brain formed first were "primitive" and less valuable, while those added last were much more sophisticated and important. A half-truth at best, this theory has kept scientists and parents alike from appreciating intelligence before birth and has justified inhumane practices at birth. If the sophisticated, "advanced" parts of the brain were not yet developed, the reasoning went, the baby could not have meaningful experiences. Memory and learning were out of the question.

The cerebral cortex, the symmetrical left- and right-brain structures lying at the top of the skull, is formed last and does have those special convolutions, the latest evolutionary wrinkles that give humans a competitive edge over other creatures. However, it was false to conclude that the cortex was not working until finished and that the rest of the brain could not engage in complex activity. Long before the completion of the cortex, complex systems for breathing, sleeping, waking, crying, spatial orientation, and movement are already functioning. The senses of taste, touch, smell, and hearing are fully operative and coordinated. Even vision is advanced at birth, although the visual portion of the cortex is not yet fully developed.

**Babies Can't Think.** Until recently, brain experts generally agreed that the newborn, like the beloved storybook character Winnie the Pooh, was "of very little brain." A recent book on the nature of the child by a noted Harvard psychologist says the cortex of the young infant resembles that of an adult rat.

With such poor equipment, how could a newborn think? Academic psychologists use big words to deny infant mental activity: presymbolic, pre-representational, prereflective. In other words, babies are without words and cannot think. This relates to another myth—that in order to think, you must have language. Recent investigations have shown that babies do a lot of thinking, with or without language. You will see evidence of this thinking when your newborn purposefully reaches out, gives an inquisitive look, frowns (or screams) in protest, gurgles in satisfaction, or gasps in excitement. Newborns also listen intently to their mothers reading stories and prefer to hear again those heard weeks before birth. And note this: they listen attentively as long as mother reads *forward,* but will stop listening as soon as she reads backward (nonsense)—another indication of good thinking.

More tellingly, infants are great dreamers, according to studies of brain waves. They dream much more than you and I do. Meticulous observation by scientists of infant body movements and facial expressions during dreaming shows that they act and look just like adults do when dreaming. How could they dream without thinking?

**No Sense of Self.**   Without physical senses and a fully furnished brain, the myth goes, there can be no sense of self and of other selves. Psychoanalysts have declared that infants are "autistic" and unresponsive to social signals; they are not ready for relationships, certainly not for communication.

"Solipsistic" was the word renowned Swiss psychologist Jean Piaget chose to describe newborns, meaning that they were out of touch with the outside world and totally preoccupied with themselves. This theory is no longer defensible. Although Piaget was a pioneering theorist in developmental psychology, he did not have the advantage of our present knowledge of newborns. He taught that it might take a newborn eighteen months to escape from being "egocentric" and to regard himself as an object among others.

Students of Piaget continue to state this view. Boston psychologist Burton White writes that newborns are helpless, cannot think, use language, socialize with another human, or even deliberately move about. He claims that for the first few weeks of life, a baby is not very interested in any aspect of the external environment.

If you accept this view, you will be discouraged from having intimate dialog with your newborn and deprived of the many gifts your baby is prepared to give you. You and your baby are *linked,* not alien from each other. Your performance is a duet, not a solo. Babies watch intently for changes in your face and can instantly mimic expressions of sadness, happiness, and surprise. Babies listen with incredible precision to adult speech. Films show that they lead as well as respond in dialog with parents.

If babies were lost in their own world, they would not be so good at analyzing and responding to sounds. They will stop eating, even when hungry, to listen to something interesting. If they hear other babies crying, they will usually be moved to cry with them. If they hear a recording of their own cry, they may suddenly stop crying—an indication that they recognize themselves.

Psychologists have been finding precursors of self-consciousness before the age of two or three, when self-awareness had been thought to begin. One authority writes that infants discover they have a mind and others have minds when they are nine months old. Child psychologist Colwyn Trevarthen of the University of Edinburgh believes that interaction between people is *innately* human and can be seen in newborns.

**Babies Don't Need Their Mothers.** This myth justifies keeping newborns in hospital nurseries and away from their mothers, a practice said to be necessary to ensure the babies' health. The opposite is true. From its mother the baby receives antibodies to ward off infections, as well as individual attention not available in a nursery. Lying next to mother helps the baby regulate its own body temperature, metabolic rate, hormone and enzyme levels, heart rate, and breathing. Separation of mothers and newborns is a physical deprivation and an emotional trial.

Mothers know deep within themselves what scientists are just discovering—that relations between mothers and babies are mutual, reciprocal, even magical. A baby's cry triggers release of the mother's milk, the only perfect milk on earth for babies. Breast-feeding after delivery speeds expulsion of the placenta and protects the mother from hemorrhaging. In addition, there is a vital power in the baby's look and touch to turn on feelings and skills necessary for successful mothering. Babies need to hear their mother's voice, learn her sleep cycles, and recognize her body odors and facial expressions. Babies need to know their mothers are all right.

**The Age Myth.** Age is a status category that works against infants. Without realizing it, we tend to discount age groups different from our own: embryo, fetus, newborn, child, adolescent, or elderly. Somehow these "others" seem woefully inferior, disabled, and incapable of being persons as we are.

Generally, younger means lower status. We think a baby is not real enough to listen to, to learn from, or to protect from inhumane treatment. The baby will become a person at some later time—perhaps when it can walk, talk, or go to school.

Myths aside, babies seem to act as individuals long before birth, engaging in spontaneous activity to suit themselves, expressing preferences for certain sounds, motions, and tastes, and reacting to danger in the womb. Once born, from Day One, they engage in many complex activities integrating sounds and sights, regulating their work and rest, and demonstrating bona fide learning. Using their communication skills they engage you in dialog, establish intimate relationships, and, without your realizing it, they begin teaching you how to be a parent.

Emotion, a language for all ages, is worn on babies' faces. We are late in acknowledging this. Watch your infant for expressions of happiness, surprise, sadness, fear, anger, disgust, interest, and distress.

## Birth Memory: A New Frontier

Perhaps the last big scientific barrier to full recognition of infants as persons will fall with acceptance of the possibility of complex personal memory at birth. Skeptical parents sometimes come to accept birth memory when they hear their two-year-olds spontaneously talking about it. Once we know that newborns are good at learning and that learning and memory go hand in hand, it is easier to accept birth memory. Some need no further convincing because they have discovered their own birth memories by one method or another. Others have discovered these memories under hypnosis or in a psychological breakthrough in therapy.

Memory contributes to self-consciousness; the two are linked just as learning and memory are linked. Without memory, experience is useless and selfhood gravely compromised.

Nowhere is the mind of a baby more surprisingly revealed than in the ability to remember birth and to recover this memory under certain circumstances as an adult. These birth memories are time capsules containing striking evidence of personality and thought.

I discovered birth memory in the course of my work as a psychologist exploring the origin of problems with the aid of hypnosis. My clients kept having memories of birth, something I had not known was possible. The memories they shared with me started me on what has turned out to be a thirteen-year adventure in study and research, resulting in scholarly papers with lots of footnotes—and this book. I had to learn about newborns themselves, the process of birth, and the complexities of memory and consciousness. In this book I share with you my most interesting discoveries.

My clients kept telling me, in considerable detail, what happened to them at birth, including the ideas they were having as babies. I found an unexpected maturity in their "baby" thoughts. Each person spoke with authority and identity. They knew and loved their parents. Their character did not appear to be age-related or developmental in any simple sense; it was there from the start.

Touched by these reports, I began (with permission) to record them; ultimately hundreds were taped, transcribed, and scrutinized. By 1980 I figured out a method to prove that the memories were reliable: comparing the memories of mother and child pairs in hypnosis.

Some persons in hypnosis remember in unusually vivid or complete detail. This ability, called hypermnesia, has been studied, admired, and doubted by experts for decades. A recent critical review of experiments in this field confirmed that hypnotized subjects do have significantly greater recall for both verbal and nonverbal material, provided it is meaningful and is obtained by a method called free recall. Studies show that memory is facilitated, too, when the remembered event contains strong images, emotions, sensations, or meaning. Memories can be spoiled, however, if the interviewer asks leading questions, suggests answers, or uses interviewing techniques that hurry and confuse the person remembering.

Narrative moment-by-moment birth reports are rare, although many people are quite capable of having them. These rather amazing stories have all the advantages of mature language, because the babies have grown up. They reveal lucid thoughts and deep feelings going on at the time of birth.

Since the first of these birth memories was shared with me in 1975, I have listened to both inspiring and depressing reports. Perhaps because I am a psychologist and people are motivated to come to me by their suffering, I have been repeatedly confronted with the hidden wounds left by hostile words, outbursts of emotion, or worrisome questions raised at birth. These psychological "birthmarks" can and should be avoided. Creative therapies are needed to deal with these birth-created problems.

I hasten to assure you that not all babies are born with psychological problems. Babies welcomed at conception, prepared for during pregnancy, and gently birthed into loving hands begin life positively. They look out at the world with immense interest and curiosity, act as if they feel safe, and make a solid connection with their parents.

Probably thousands of adults have deliberately encountered their own birth or prebirth memories with help from a "rebirther," a "primal" therapist, or a dianetics "auditor." A smaller number have stumbled upon birth memories while in some altered state of consciousness: a psychedelic state, dream, fantasy, or meditation. A few adults claim they have always remembered parts of their birth, although they have been shy about saying so for fear of ridicule. As the climate of acceptance for birth memory warms up, more of these adults are coming forward. If you are one of them, I would like you to write down your birth memory and send it to me.

Until now, the coherent, moment-by-moment narratives of birth that can be obtained in hypnosis have been known mainly to a small circle of professionals. These narratives are presented here to the general public for the first time, with the generous permission of the men, women, and children involved. Verbatim reports have been edited for brevity, duplication, and grammar; and, for easier reading, my own words in the sessions have been deleted.

In their birth memories, "babies" now grown up describe what they experienced during labor, how they were treated by nurses and doctors, and what their parents said and did. Such memories trouble parents, stir up controversy among scientists, and cannot always be explained within the limited framework of present knowledge.

What we find in birth memories is consistent with what is found in modern research: the newborn brain, nervous system, and physical senses are active and coordinated; a normal range of human emotions is felt and expressed while the infant mind is alert, perceptive, exploring, and busy incorporating each new experience.

As long as babies were considered senseless and mindless,

memory was logically impossible and the evidence for it was set aside. This skepticism has prevailed right up to the present. Professional publications in psychology and hypnosis have been reluctant to print articles on birth memory; as a result, Americans working in this field have sometimes published their work abroad because of the more receptive climate there.

In Vienna in 1971, European psychologists and physicians established a professional association and publication (in German) specifically devoted to prenatal psychology—the International Society for Study of Prenatal Psychology (ISPP). In 1983, because there was no room for papers and symposia on prenatal or birth psychology in the major established professional societies, researchers in Canada and the United States joined in organizing the Pre and Perinatal Psychology Association of North America (PPPANA). I was one of them. At the first meeting of this new group, five hundred people heard fifty-five speakers from nine countries. Similar congresses have been convened every two years since.

Thanks to overwhelming proof of infant abilities and to impressive advances in understanding the brain, mind, and consciousness, we are now in a position to evaluate birth memories more sympathetically. Birth memories deserve close attention. What we learn from them can change how we live our lives, how we approach parenthood, conception, pregnancy, and childbirth, and how we educate each other. Some birth memories violate cherished scientific beliefs and parental expectations. For those who listen carefully, they tell us much about the difference between brain and mind, about the nasty consequences of birth trauma, and, perhaps most important of all, about new dimensions of human consciousness.

Birth reports are mini documentaries, private stories which have public significance. After listening to so many of them, I understand how beginnings can be marred, sacred moments spoiled, and obstacles left to cause frustration and misery. A bad birth can be like a thorn in the flesh which keeps getting inflamed. Birth reports also reveal the quality of life attained by mothers and fathers and the virtuous character of professional helpers. These reports remind us that safe, meaningful birth is no accident; it is a "blessed" event inspiring everyone involved.

During the twentieth century, the place of birth has shifted abruptly from home to hospital. What was always a family event has become a medical event. The psychological quality of birth has suffered. Babies dramatize this in their birth memories. Considering their testimony, we are tardy in recognizing the potential negative effects of birth on body and mind. We must awaken to the need for *good* birth.

You may not be prepared for the wisdom and maturity shown in birth reports. In depth and quality, the things on a baby's mind go far beyond anything predicted by their chronological age or the physical status of their brain. This is why some find birth memory impossible to believe. Yet the evidence mounts. Old myths, which for so long have doomed babies to inferior status, are challenged here.

As you read this book, it may dawn slowly in your consciousness that this new pool of information about newborns is not just about *them*. In a circular way, it is vital information about *us*—a window through which we can glimpse what makes us persons. Something in these pages may cause you to wonder how your own birth has influenced you. Although this book is about babies, not therapy, the reader will find hints about the connection between birth and later life at various places in the text and some referral possibilities in the section on Sources and Readings.

As you read about the maturity of the newborn and the development of life before birth, you may inevitably wonder what effect this all has on the issue of abortion. For readers who wish to know my personal beliefs and sympathies, I have made brief comments in Appendix I. Similarly,

I know how prone parents are to worry or to blame themselves for the damage they may have done their children by their actions during pregnancy and birth. I direct some words of comfort and caution to them in Appendix II.

Ahead you will find reports of happy and unhappy birthdays. You will encounter wisdom coming "out of the mouths of babes" and virtue that seems to have no relationship to age. Perhaps the information will surprise you, stir up curiosity about yourself, confirm secret hunches you have about babies, and add to your reverence for life.

# PART ONE

# *Your Extraordinary Newborn*

## CHAPTER 1

# Growing a Body and Brain

**W**omen have been growing babies from the beginning of the human race, but never with the inner vision that is possible today. No longer is the growth that takes place in a dark womb bathed in mystery and veiled from understanding. Through many "windows" opened by science, you can see what is going on inside.

One window, opened by embryology, lets you see what parts of the baby are developing by the day, week, and month. This tells you what you are building at any given time. The timetable of baby growth in the womb is full of surprises; knowing about them will help you be more deliberate in what you do for your baby.

Through another window, opened by neuroscientists and biochemists, you can look at the brain in a new way and understand how it is possible for your baby to show many signs of intelligence long before birth. This knowledge can help you understand yourself as well as your baby. New information suggests that mothers and fathers do not have to *wait* to have meaningful interaction with the unborn. The key to communication with the silent womb is knowledge of what is going on there.

## The Magic of Conception

LeAnn had been charting her temperature and fertility cycles on the calendar. One night after she and her husband made love, as she lay dimly awake before falling asleep, she had the distinct impression of something spiritual happening to her body. When she woke the next morning she announced, "Well, we have our baby." She circled the date on the calendar and wrote "conceived" over it. She said the feeling was unique and definite. It turned out to be right.

How could any woman *feel* conception? The process is infinitesimal and fragile. About two weeks after menstruation, a single egg awaits the arrival of a maelstrom of sperm during intercourse. Although the 200 million sperm that have been launched seem frantic to get there, the scanning electron microscope shows that once they touch the egg they go into an extended "hug" until one of them is drawn in. The egg cell membrane then changes to seal out all other sperm. If this process is successful, as it is about 40 percent of the time, pregnancy begins.

In the first twenty-four hours after the sperm unites with the egg, the fertilized cell divides in two. This happens again and again in a process of transformation and differentiation of cells, until there are several hundred billion cells organized into all the bodily structures and organs of the baby. Photos now record the stages of growth for all parts of the body.

Within ten days of conception, this tiny cluster of multiplying cells (called a blastocyst), barely visible to the naked eye, has made a slow journey to the womb. Here the favored blastocyst—again, about 40 percent succeed—will find a secure lodging place in the lining of the womb.

After only three weeks, the embryo has a head and tail, swims in fluid inside the shock-absorbing amniotic sac, and develops segments that eventually will form into brain and spinal cord. In the fourth week, the beginnings of the heart, blood circulation, and digestive tract have begun to grow. Arms and legs begin to bud out in the fifth week. Already the heart starts pumping blood, even as it is undergoing construction from one chamber into four, complete with interconnecting valves, all of which will be in place at two months.

While you may still be wondering whether you are pregnant, the brain, eyes, liver, and ears are developing. Six weeks old and only three-fifths of an inch long, the embryo is floating securely in its silvery sac. At seven weeks the face, eyes, nose, lips, and tongue are visible, along with the earliest signs of teeth and bone. By the eighth week, fingers and hands are well defined, toe joints are clear, and muscle movement begins. By the tenth week, all the basic structures of the body are in place.

## The Baby's Nervous System

The first evidence that the preborn's nervous system is working is found in the activation of the heart muscle at five weeks and in measurable electrical activity in the brain at six weeks.

Barely two months after conception, the baby will react to strokes of a fine hair around its cheeks by moving its head away, bending its trunk and pelvis, and extending arms and shoulders enough to push the hair away. Although this movement has usually been described as a reflex, I think the reaction is best understood as the first sensitivity to touch.

From the time of this first reaction to a stroke on the cheek, sensitivity in all parts of the body progresses, as documented by scientists around the world. In America, proof of these sensitivities has been available since scientists at the University of Pittsburgh began recording them in motion pictures in 1932.

Not surprisingly, the baby's face is the area that reacts most during the first few months, beginning with movements of the mouth, lips, and tongue and swallowing. All through life our faces are sensitive, attentive, and expressive. Squinting and sneering expressions have been filmed at fourteen weeks after conception. Since these expressions have often come in response to invasive disturbances of the womb, it is possible that they represent meaningful reactions to what is happening at the time. Puckering of the lips, scowling, and muscle tension around the eyes have been associated with audible crying as early as the sixth month of pregnancy. Appropriate facial and vocal expressions imply that some kind of "central intelligence agency" is already linking body and brain.

The face is not the only area of nervous activity early in womb life. The genital area responds to stroking at ten weeks, the palms at eleven weeks, the soles of the feet at twelve weeks. These are the important surface areas that eventually will have the greatest number and variety of nerve cells in the adult.

By eleven weeks a baby's arms and legs are sensitive to hair strokes. By fifteen to seventeen weeks, so are the abdomen and buttocks. If you could reach in and touch your unborn, you would find that virtually all parts of the body respond to light touch by seventeen weeks.

## Rapid Growth

The preborn grows rapidly, expanding and perfecting its basic structures and developing more complex interconnections of blood vessels and nerves. Three months after conception, eyes and ears move into proper position and the skeleton is clearly defined. Hands are brought together, and thumb-sucking may commence (by birth some babies have a little callus on their thumb to show for it). The baby's respiratory tract, which starts at the nose and branches again and again on the way to the lungs, will be ready for the first breathing movements.

In another month your preborn, five to six inches long, will have a fully formed mouth and lips and breathe amniotic fluid in and out through its mouth. This liquid breathing guarantees that when the fluid is replaced with air at birth, the respiratory muscles will be well developed and capable of prolonged work without fatigue. The tiny sacs that store air in the lungs will increase in number and size throughout pregnancy and for eight years after birth, one reason children need plenty of fresh, clean air to breathe.

During womb life, your baby's liquid breathing will be speeded up or slowed down by your intake of nicotine, caffeine, alcohol, or other drugs. Measurements by doctors indicate that slowed breathing is a negative factor in a baby's health. Fast breathing, which happens when the mother smokes, is considered a strained effort by the baby to get enough oxygen. These facts indicate that breathing is one of the first behaviors to be influenced by the mother's lifestyle and culture.

By the twentieth week, the halfway point in growth, the preborn is approaching a foot in length and a pound in weight. Eyelids and brows are well developed and the body starts to fatten. You begin to notice that you are becoming more round. With an ear to the abdomen, a father may be able to hear the baby's heartbeat. At about this time, you may also be able to feel the differences between hands, feet, head, and buttocks as your baby kicks, jumps, and turns. Strange little rhythmic jolts periodically announce that the baby is having hiccups.

Over the next three months the baby becomes much heavier. A protective padding of fat develops in the eighth month to help keep the baby warm after birth. The baby's kicks are now impressive. By the ninth month, quarters are cramped and you may see the movement of arms and legs in the bulge creeping across your tummy.

In these last months your body is pumping the baby full of antibodies, the disease-fighting proteins you have built up over many years. This is a gift that will go on giving, as a daughter eventually passes them on to the next generation. More antibodies will be transferred in the watery colostrum that comes in before breast milk. In addition, the placenta produces gamma globulin for you as well as your baby, affording extra protection from diseases in the last trimester and after birth.

Approaching forty weeks, your baby shows clearer waking and sleeping rhythms and a more definite cry. Measurement of brain waves during this last trimester shows more organization, steadier activity, and greater synchrony between the left and right halves of the brain.

Finally, at around the fortieth week, your preborn will send a hormone signal (one that scientists would like to know more about) to your body calling for an end to the pregnancy. The uterine contractions you feel tell you that labor has begun.

## Prenatal Exercise

Less than two months after conception, the part of the baby's nervous system that has to do with gravity and balance in space—the vestibular system—begins to form. It is this system that assures synchrony between your movements and the baby's. If you stand on your head or go dancing, your baby will sense the changes in position, speed, and direction and attempt to stabilize itself. If you are jumping around, your baby will be jumping around, too, whether it likes it or not.

Apart from adjusting to your movements, your tiny preborn uses its vestibular system to begin its own program of body-building. Long before you can feel it, your preborn is engaging in regular exercise and stopping for brief rests. Between ten and twelve weeks there is a sudden spurt of activity: rolling from side to side, extension and then flexion of the back and neck, waving of arms, and kicking of legs. The feet flex and extend in a swift kick of the side wall of the gestation sac.

All muscles of the preborn seem to be brought into play

during these "training sessions," say the doctors in Johannesburg, South Africa, who studied this activity in forty-six pregnant women. The longest "exerciser" did seven and a half minutes straight; the longest "rester" rested only five and a half minutes.

Dutch scientists say that because these gyrations are graceful, voluntary, and spontaneous, they are an early example of initiative and self-expression on the part of the preborn. (You may appreciate knowing that *you* are not in charge of everything and that your preborn has an agenda all its own!) Hidden in these creative gymnastics is evidence of brain-mind cooperation, not expected so early.

## Brain Growth

The brain is most of what is crowded into your head. It is not a single organ but a complex group of organs with various abilities. What makes them particularly hard to understand is that the parts operate together by means of elaborate interconnections. Though much has been learned, many mysteries and paradoxes still surround the workings of these parts.

Here is how your preborn's brain develops: About three weeks after conception, the basic parts of the spinal cord and brain begin to appear. By the twelfth week they are in place. The top end of the spinal cord blossoms into the brainstem, the lower portion of the brain, which grows rapidly through the first seven weeks. Growing out of that, a little higher up, the midbrain and forebrain are expanding. The wrinkled outer surface of the forebrain is the cerebral cortex, the latest evolutionary accomplishment of the human brain. The distinctive wrinkles and convolutions of the cortex are no accident. This ingenious design allows for many more brain cells (neurons) to be packed into a limited space.

Depending on conditions, the preborn's brain cells keep multiplying and growing until there are between 20 and 200 billion. Scientists generally believe that having more of these working units gives the baby the advantage of greater information storage and exchange. Brain cells come in various forms but have characteristic branches (dendrites) and long stems (axons) that make them look like uprooted trees. The branches reach out to neighboring cells forming communication junctions (synapses). Chemical miracles happen here as neurotransmitters exchange "messages." These exotic chemicals are contained in little knobs, as many as fifty thousand of them in a single cell of cortex. In spite of this vast complexity, signals speed back and forth through this lacy network of nerves and arrive at the right muscles, glands, and organs in an orderly, timely way.

For the past fifty years, experts have doubted the efficiency of these nerve transmissions in the preborn and newborn. Their doubt was based on the tardy development of myelin, a fatty insulating sheath that eventually surrounds all nerves. The belief was that unmyelinated nerves could not transmit messages efficiently. Leaning heavily on this assumption, experts dismissed many discoveries about the talents of newborns.

The fact is, myelination progresses gradually and varies greatly throughout the nervous system. While it is largely incomplete at birth, that doesn't seem to matter; some nerves are not completely insulated until puberty, long after the brain has reached an advanced stage of development. Considering the many abilities that have been verified both before and after birth, it appears that myelination is irrelevant.

For most of the past century, scientists have valued the parts of the brain according to their arrival time and location; parts close to the tail and grown first (brainstem) have been considered somehow inferior to the higher portions that are finished last (cortex). It was presumed that without the cortex, the preborn could not find meaning in experience. Doctors were sure that babies could not know, learn, or remember any of the things that happen to them in the womb or at birth. Routine obstetrical practices were built on this belief.

The cerebral cortex of the preborn has been the subject of intense investigation to determine just when it is complete and presumably ready to work. Scientists judge its maturity by the presence of dendrites and dendrite spines, the nerve branches that receive the information pouring in from all over the body. Using electron microscopes, they found dendrites and dendrite spines in place between twenty and twenty-eight weeks of pregnancy. So it is no longer correct to claim that preborns and newborns lack higher brain centers. These structures continue to expand in number and complexity until birth and after birth as well.

Further proof that the preborn's cortex is working comes from measurement of brain waves. These show that the brain responds to stimulation of vision, touch, and hearing no later than the end of the seventh month of pregnancy. This supports the assumption that even in the womb, your baby is capable of responding meaningfully to experience.

What these measures do not explain are the many signs of intelligence that have been found much earlier in fetal life.

The failure of brain experts to anticipate the competence of unborn and newborn babies has led to new theories about the brain and its relationship to the body. The new theories are encouraging to parents and others trying to decide if a baby can listen, suffer, or learn anything in the womb or in the delivery room. According to Australian neurosurgeon Richard Bergland, the brain is itself a giant *gland* because it produces hormones, contains receptors for hormones produced elsewhere in the body, is bathed in hormones, and has hormones running up and down the fibers of individual nerves. Hence the new designation, the *wet* brain. The significance of this for the unborn is that it changes all the chronologies about when the "brain" starts working.

One of the exciting discoveries about this new "fluid" brain is that many vital parts of the body's intelligence system lie entirely outside the head. This communication network has been uncovered by the use of radioactive molecules. It was discovered that particular hormones fit particular receptors like keys fit locks. At the National Institute of Mental Health, Candace Pert and colleagues have mapped the receptor sites for fifty or more neuropeptides, the amino-acid compounds produced directly by nerve cells. These important juices have an information function as they move back and forth through virtually all body fluids. Other molecular messengers between brain and body move up and down via nerve conduits.

Knowing the actual places in the brain and body where particular messengers are traveling allows Pert to state with authority that neuropeptides link three systems: (1) the nervous system (brain, spinal cord, and senses); (2) the endocrine system (hormones); and (3) the immune system (spleen, bone marrow, lymph nodes, and the other special cells that fight disease). This adds up to one big intelligence network where the conversation is both to and from the brain.

Parents and babies alike have a stake in the intelligence of the immune system. Unlike brain structures which are fixed in location, cells of the immune system actually *move* through the body recognizing and digesting tumorous growths and foreign matter, repairing wounds, and fighting disease in collaboration with neuropeptides. They are not only equipped with receptor sites for neuropeptides but they are smart; they can *manufacture* neuropeptides and other chemicals which affect bodily health and emotions. Among other things, immune cells can make endorphins, the body's own natural "pleasure molecules" (opiates). Pert says, "I can't separate the brain from body."

This pioneering work has shifted attention from nerve synapses as the critical junction for information processing, to receptor sites throughout the preborn's body and brain where information is received from neuropeptides. Pleasurable beta-endorphins, manufactured mainly in the pituitary gland, are found in the bloodstream starting in the seventh week of pregnancy. By the twelfth week, pituitary processing of these substances is similar to that found in adults. Other peptides have been recognized throughout the second trimester. The hypothalamus portion of the brain (intimately connected to the pituitary gland) appears to be fully grown in less than four months. Researchers presume that the presence of these substances and structures has a purpose and that they probably function whenever present.

Most significant for the question of awareness in the preborn is the discovery of thick clusters of neuropeptide receptors in the brainstem—so many, in fact, that Pert believes this makes the brainstem part of the limbic system, the portion of the brain primarily involved in emotion and memory. Since the brainstem is one of the earliest parts of the brain to grow, this discovery forms a new basis for memory in the first trimester of pregnancy.

## Nurturing the Brain

Brain growth proceeds in spurts throughout pregnancy and continues for years after birth. Parents have a lot to do with the quality of this growth. One of the myths formerly taught by experts on pregnancy was that "malnutrition spares the brain"—that is, even if the mother is poorly nourished, the baby's brain receives priority treatment from the body. Only in the last quarter of the twentieth century has this wishful theory been discredited.

Many studies now show that prenatal malnutrition results in babies with brains of lower weight, length, and size. All parts of the shrunken brain suffer: neurons, synapses, neurotransmitters, and myelin. Malnutrition strikes the preborn's liver most severely, and it is the liver that manufactures glucose, which fuels the brain. The undersized liver struggles to supply a brain that needs more than twice the supply of glucose it can produce.

When mothers eat properly during pregnancy, they are making a vital gift to their babies: a fully grown brain.

Construction of your baby's body and brain can also be impaired by a variety of toxic chemicals, drugs, viruses, and pollutants known collectively as teratogens (substances capable of producing fetal malformations). This problem is so serious that some states and counties have established teratogen registries to provide information about drugs, chemicals, and other physical agents that may be harmful to the preborn. Books are also available for guidance. The subject is too broad to go into detail here, but both fathers and mothers should realize that they may be exposed to toxic chemicals in the workplace that can cause infertility or birth defects.

Drugs, prescribed or unprescribed, may be hazardous to the preborn. One of the most common teratogens is alcohol. Even in ancient Greece, Plato warned parents that their drunkenness would result in children who were inferior. Modern research has proved him right. One study with alarming implications for parents shows that alcohol intake around the time of *conception* can be devastating. Drinking at this time has a greater risk for malformations of the eyes, ears, lips, head, and face.

## The Active Prenate

From a mother's point of view, signs of intelligent life inside are subtle. The little kicks you feel between sixteen and twenty-two weeks of pregnancy, sometimes referred to as "quickening," are not really the first movements, merely the first ones you can feel. New Zealand's Sir William Liley, a pioneer in the field of fetal research, has explained that the uterus, like most internal organs, is insensitive to touch but when movements stretch the wall of the uterus, the feeling is picked up by the abdominal wall.

Your preborn feels many things and is busy keeping comfortable inside. Constantly shifting position to keep up with you, the preborn will avoid any sustained pressure from an instrument that the doctor puts on your abdomen and will pull away from anything pushing on a prominent part. Liley found out how active and sensitive these little bodies are when he was trying to develop diagnostic and medical treatments for them in utero. Virtually all movements of the mother caused a movement of the fetus. Before they could work on an unborn baby, the mother had to lie still for fifteen minutes to allow the fetus to settle down. Then the doctors had to avoid any last-minute touching of the abdomen, or the fetus would shift again and spoil their aim.

In the first half of pregnancy, the womb space is relatively large and globular. The microclimate inside is warm and humid, the baby's mood a drowsy wakefulness alternating with activity. The temperature is a point or so higher than yours, and if you have a fever, your baby will have one, too. The volume of amniotic fluid reaches its maximum between twenty-eight and thirty-two weeks of pregnancy, and until that time the passenger can lie well stretched out. From then on, with decreasing fluid and increasing body bulk, comfort becomes more of a challenge.

As your womb becomes narrower on one end and your prenate grows longer, it is generally corraled into a longitudinal lie. Depending on whether the preborn prefers to flex or extend its knees, different ends of the womb will be preferred. Liley discovered that babies move from one end of the uterus to the other by propelling themselves with feet and legs. Changing sides, however, requires a longitudinal spiral roll and at the midpoint a 180-degree twist of the spine.

Liley's films show this prenatal ballet movement beginning with extension and rotation of the head. Next the shoulders rotate. Finally the lumbar spine and legs rotate using long spinal muscles. This has been seen as early as the twenty-sixth week and is a feat that cannot be duplicated outside the womb for two or three weeks after full-term birth. This demonstrates the unique advantages of the water environment of the womb that provides the unborn with months of relatively easy opportunities for activity and self-expression. In all such moves, superb coordination of the brain and body cannot be denied.

Your baby's body, fully prepared for birth, is designed with very flexible and fluid intervertebral disks and joints ready for folding into tight places. Head plates guarding the brain will yield to pressure by overlapping, then slowly expand back to normal. You have grown a baby who is prepared for a safe journey through the birth canal.

# CHAPTER 2

## *Alert and Aware*

*N*ewborns have had a long, long struggle to convince us of their ability to feel, taste, smell, hear, and see. Mothers through the ages have probably been more ready to believe them than fathers, and fathers more ready than doctors. Newborns seem pitifully small and unfinished, obviously ill-equipped, but their size and sleepiness are misleading. Drugged or partially drugged, they are even more misleading.

While you are getting acquainted with your newborn, your baby will be getting acquainted with *you,* and by the same means: the senses. It may come as a surprise to learn that your baby will do this about as well as you do. This is new knowledge that has been difficult to gain; and for many it may be difficult to accept.

In 1891 psychologist William James assumed that newborn babies were "so assailed by eyes, ears, nose, skin, and entrails at once" that they must experience the world as "one great blooming, buzzing confusion." This view was not derived from research about infants—something not available at the time—but from an easy logic that most people accepted. If you consider that similar false views prevailed for thousands of years before James and for nearly a century afterward, you will have an idea of what babies have been up against.

In the last hundred years, expert opinion held that baby brains were not yet grown and therefore not much use at birth. Parents might think their babies were adorable but had to accept the fact that they were stupid. Scientists had no interest in studying newborn senses when they believed the newborn's brain lacked the ability to coordinate and interpret them.

Today, in spite of abundant new knowledge about infant senses, you may find that even obstetricians remain doubtful. Birth practices remain much the same: bright lights, cold rooms, procedures that are painful for the baby. Too often professionals blunder through birth violating a baby's senses, believing those senses don't exist. Parents are in danger of blundering through pregnancy, unaware that the preborn's senses are already working.

Prenates come to their senses gradually and quietly in the womb. Sensitivity to touch progresses rather quickly from the face area around eight weeks from conception to virtually all skin areas by seventeen weeks.

When you are ten to twelve weeks pregnant, your preborn begins regular exercises demonstrating that senses connected with muscle, tendon, and joint movement are functioning smoothly. Some mechanisms of balance are also demonstrated at this time, and all parts of the system registering your baby's head and body motion and the pull of gravity are full grown about halfway through pregnancy.

## Sensing Temperature Changes

Your baby's thermal senses are revealed in reactions to extremes of hot and cold in the womb, although general temperature regulation is determined by the mother. During pregnancy your baby's temperature is a degree or two higher than yours. True self-regulation of body temperature takes the newborn about a week to develop. This means that the sudden plunge of the baby into a cold hospital delivery room will be a shock.

Research shows that the newborn's body temperature is best regulated when the baby is kept in close contact with its mother. Babies don't sweat or pant to control excessive heat, but their skin reddens, they become less active, fall asleep, and stretch out into a "sunbathing" posture—all to aid in cooling. Babies react adeptly to sharply raised or lowered temperatures by adjusting their intake of calories per day. Remarkably, during a ten-degree rise or fall of temperature in their surroundings, babies adjust the relative percentages of milk and water they drink, while holding to the same total volume of fluid intake.

Taste and hearing are developed early in pregnancy and are used by your baby for *months* before birth. Smell and sight are senses ready to use *at* birth.

## Tasting

Tasting is one of the basic ways we find out about the things around us. Babies do it all the time. You have to watch them closely because *anything* can end up in the mouth. They practiced doing this in the womb.

Your baby's ability to taste is made possible by about five thousand taste buds, made up of fifty or so taste cells found on the rough surface of the tongue and adjoining structures. These taste cells connect with the brainstem via two nerves that serve areas around the face and mouth. The timetable for development of all the delicate structures used in tasting (taste cells, buds, pores, and microvilli) has been uncovered by microscopic research.

Taste buds start appearing at eight weeks and reach adult form by Week 13. In one more week they are surrounded by the pores and hairlike microvilli cells that complete the system. No essential changes take place in these receptors after this time period, except that they multiply in number and spread themselves more widely. It seems likely from this evidence that taste buds are working by fifteen weeks.

Other studies show that your prenate begins swallowing by twelve weeks. Putting it all together, scientists believe that your baby is having taste experiences for about twenty-five weeks *before* birth. What they are mainly tasting during this time is the amniotic fluid that surrounds them. This fluid is quite complex and may be a "gustatorial" challenge. The snacks available within this silvery commissary are such things as glucose; fructose; lactic, pyruvic, and citric acids; fatty acids; phospholipids; creatinine; urea; uric acid; amino acids; polypeptides; proteins; salts; and other natural products. We can only guess the taste of this organic fare. In addition, as sonograms and intrauterine photos show, babies in the womb suck on their fingers, hands, and toes.

Studies using radioactive tracers show prenates drinking from 15 to 40 milliliters of amniotic fluid per hour in the third trimester. In nourishment this adds up to 40 calories a day, if swallowing is normal. Large well-nourished babies swallow at a high rate and small, grossly malnourished babies at a very low rate.

When a bitter-tasting substance is injected into the amniotic fluid, babies suddenly stop drinking it. Conversely, if saccharine is injected, some babies will double their swallowing. Alcohol and nicotine seem to suppress appetite; babies exposed to these by their mothers are lower weight at birth. Regular maternal drinking and smoking usually results in small, underweight babies, who are at greater risk of illness and death in the first years of life.

After birth, your baby will have definite taste preferences. Something babies have in common with many adults is a "sweet tooth." Sucking activity will usually increase with presentation of sweet fluids, but bitter and sour tastes have the opposite effect. When compared to adult reactions to these tastes, infants seem to react less strongly to bitter and more strongly to sour, raising the possibility that some of your baby's senses may be more acute than yours. When presented with a range of natural sugars, infants choose sucrose and fructose over glucose and lactose, meaning the sweeter it is the better they like it. This means you don't have to teach your baby to like sweets but you may have to hold the sweets to give other tastes a chance.

To find out how discriminating newborn taste buds are, psychologist Lewis Lipsitt and colleagues at Brown University designed a special crib controlled for light and sound and where sucking, respiration, and heart activity were continually monitored by polygraph devices. They invented a "suckometer" to measure sucking activity and pressure, and a special nipple and pump apparatus to deliver measured drops of fluids. With great precision they offered babies various tastes and combinations of tastes. Instruments told them when sucking speeded up or slowed down, contained longer or shorter rest periods, and when a baby invested more sucks in each burst of sucking.

The results: newborn babies are sharply and critically responsive to the slightest alterations in the chemical content of fluids reaching the tongue. Distinctive sucking patterns for different fluids were definitely related to the taste of these fluids.

In these experiments with taste, infants remembered and learned quickly from experience. For example, infants who sucked more times per minute to get sweet fluids would immediately suck less if given plain water. One taste experience affects the next. Not aware of this, nurses may confuse babies with sweet water and formula drinks when they are breast-feeding.

In one experiment, drops of either plain water, mildly sweet, or mildly salty water were administered one drop at a time, while the length of the following sucking burst was measured. Newborns quickly detected the sweet drops and sucked longer, sucked shorter for plain water, and much shorter for the salty drops. They detected salt at extremely low concentrations.

Other experiments reveal that you can rely on your baby's facial expressions to tell you how something tastes. In a series of experiments at Hebrew University in Jerusalem, psychologist Jacob Steiner presented sweet, sour, and bitter tastes to newborns, photographed their reactions, and then asked independent observers to judge which babies had been given which substances. Reactions to these tastes were correctly and consistently identified on the basis of facial expressions alone.

All human beings seem similar in their facial reactions to sharply different tastes. Steiner found this out by trying various tastes on premature babies, blind babies, and adults. In all cases, sour inspired puckering of the lips, bitter evoked retching or spitting, and sweet tastes generated looks of enjoyment and satisfaction.

## The Sense of Hearing

Hearing is the sonic link between you and your baby, a bridge for learning and communication with the big world out there. The detection of sound makes possible the birth of speech. To be deprived of hearing is a grave setback, to be endowed with it, an infinite adventure. During gestation, hearing is like a private telephone line enabling family conversations long before birth.

Signs of ear development can be seen in your prenate only a week after conception. By the halfway mark of pregnancy, elaborate labyrinths, chambers, and passageways with impressive nerve and brain connections are in place. The cochlear nerve, which is directly involved in hearing, gets its myelin insulation early, and the temporal lobe of the brain, to which the ear sends its data, will be fully myelinated by birth. Since other parts of the baby's brain and nervous system are only partially insulated at birth, it seems that hearing has a very high priority.

French hearing pioneer Alfred Tomatis points out that the special sensory cells that are packed so densely in the ear, called cells of Corti, are similar to the cells found in the skin. This makes it possible to think of the Corti cells of the ear as a kind of skin—or, even more exciting, to view the skin as an extension of the ear—the *skin* as a very great ear!

Information reaches the ear by two other routes, air conduction and bone conduction, so we can think of the whole skeleton as a receiving dish that helps to focus sound.

Researchers believe babies begin hearing as early as the eighteenth week of pregnancy. By the twenty-eighth week, the baby's responses to sound are so consistent that functional, interactive hearing seems sure.

One of the earliest proven signs of hearing involved the playing of music in a London maternity hospital to preborns between four and five months. Beethoven, Brahms, and hard-rock music made them restless; Vivaldi and Mozart calmed them.

Many pregnant mothers have stories to tell about the reaction of their unborn to sound. In Essex, England, a pregnant woman attended a very loud rock concert. The baby kicked so hard that the mother came home with a broken rib. Another couple remembers how wildly their baby kicked during the movie thriller, *Raiders of the Lost Ark.* In the womb, my own grandson reacted so strongly to a movie about the Vietnam war that his mother had to leave the theater. Preborns seem to be telling us they can hear loud sounds and don't like them. They are not asking for silence, in my opinion, but at least for more peace and harmony.

Other evidence of fetal hearing comes from a high-tech study of the earliest infant cries. In 1955 American child-language specialist Henry Truby joined an international team in Stockholm to analyze infant cries using the latest acoustical inventions. One device broke sound into four thousand parts per second. A spectrograph produced elaborately detailed sound portraits, "cryprints," having as much individual quality as fingerprints.

Similarities in sound patterns identified an individual and his group. From these and X-ray motion pictures, they discovered that babies in the womb were not only hearing, but apparently *learning* speech and "practicing" the fine neuro-muscular movements of the vocal tract that are used in cry-ing and vocalizing after birth.

In the cryprints of premature infants five months old, weighing only 900 grams, they found a correspondence to intonations, rhythms, and other speech performance fea-tures of the mother. This revolutionary discovery meant not only that the infants were hearing their mothers but had been taking language lessons. The unborn babies had al-ready acquired some of their mothers' personal accents and speech sounds.

Prenates with normal hearing react to tones beamed to them in the womb; those found to be deaf at birth do not respond to these tones in utero. Prenates may become sound-deprived in the womb if their mothers are mute, deaf, or quiet and withdrawn. At birth these babies cry strangely or not at all, revealing that they missed out on their speech lessons.

There are several reasons why a mother's voice turns out to be so important to her baby. During womb life, the baby is better equipped to hear the high-pitched voice of the mother than the low-pitched voice of the father. Dr. Toma-tis explains that the areas for hearing high-frequency sounds are well developed before birth, while those for lower fre-quencies will not be fully tuned until puberty. This surpris-ing fact accounts for the way male voices drop about an octave and female voices drop a few notes at that time— another example of how hearing affects speaking.

A second reason the mother's voice is favored over that of the father is that the preborn hears more by bone conduc-tion than by air conduction; the womb is a sound chamber. To be heard, fathers must make special efforts. To use that bone and nerve reception network, dads need to get in close, speak clearly, and talk a little higher than usual.

The preborn is never beyond the range of mother's voice.

Your voice is a constant; your preborn bathes in it. This may be a heavy responsibility. Who else has to hear *all* your sounds day and night? Dr. Tomatis warns mothers that the earliest experiences of sound in the womb can have a stimulating or discouraging effect on your baby's desire to listen and communicate. In extreme cases where the womb is a noise box, a baby may want to hide from life. If your voice is chronically shrill, angry, and alarming, it is possible that your preborn will learn to dread it. Try humming, singing, crooning, and speaking softly. Similar advice should be followed by fathers for similar reasons. Your relationship with your child starts with that private line to the womb.

Of course, there are other sounds to think about. Sudden noise in a quiet room can startle your preborn; you can see this on ultrasound imaging machines. At twenty-five weeks, your baby may surprise you by jumping in reaction to kettledrums at a concert. Tones broadcast to the preborn send its heart rate up and get its body moving, something discovered in 1947 by Lester Sontag, one of the pioneers in studying the behavior of babies in the womb.

Your abdomen itself provides a certain amount of sonic entertainment. The loudest inside sounds to reach your prenate are probably from your stomach and bowels, peaking at 85 decibels. Sounds heard at 55 decibels or so include the all-pervading rumble of blood in the great arteries supplying the uterus and placenta, moving in synchrony with your heart. Today, phonograph records, toy bears, and even therapeutic chambers re-create these sounds of the womb. They have unique value and potency for your newborn.

After studying hundreds of statues and paintings of madonnas, psychologist Lee Salk reported that 80 percent of them show the child held on the mother's left side. He thinks this might be an intuitive acknowledgment of the sound newborns know best and remember fondly. Your baby will seem to receive special comfort when held on the left side of your chest, over the heart. This may also explain why babies tend to be calmed by the slow ticking of a grandfather's clock, or soothed by a metronome going fifty to ninety beats per minute.

Salk conducted a famous experiment playing heartbeat sounds in a hospital nursery. He kept track of the babies' food intake and weight gain. One group of newborns heard the broadcast of heartbeats at the normal rate of seventy-two beats per minute. He recorded their audible reactions by microphone. Salk compared the results with a similar group that did not hear the heart sounds. On the same amount of food, seventy percent of the infants in the heartbeat group gained more weight; they also slept better and cried less. Did all these good things happen because they were reminded of their mothers?

An interesting footnote on the Salk study: For a while, he tried broadcasting a racing heartbeat of 128 beats per minute. The babies couldn't stand it. They got so upset that this part of the experiment had to be stopped.

As you might expect, given all this, your baby is equipped to hear very well at birth. In fact, normal newborns hear about as well as adults, as shown by measurements of hearing by means of brainstem electric response audiometry (BERA). Newborns even track the smallest units of sound (phonemes) better than adults do. Judging from cardiac measurements in response to sound, infant hearing appears to extend as low as 40 decibels. Sounds may have to last longer than 300 milliseconds to register with a newborn, but many sounds in a baby's natural environment are within these parameters.

Your newborn can judge the location of sound and will turn toward it with the expectation of seeing something. This deceptively simple act actually involves the complex coordination of three sensory systems: sound, movement, and sight. Infants can respond to sounds presented from left and right but are especially good at detecting straight-ahead sounds, leading one researcher to conclude that this ability must be innate.

Even during sleep, a baby is hearing sounds, according to one study using brain-wave measurements. If you wait until the baby is asleep to fight with your spouse, you may be kidding yourself but not the baby. Simple clicking sounds broadcast at 60 decibels were picked up by the newborn's brain during both active and quiet stages of sleep.

Your baby also arrives equipped with the ability to interpret crying sounds. Newborns can tell the difference between recordings of real babies crying, white noise (a nondescript static noise), and computer-simulated cries. Babies are typically more disturbed by genuine cries and most disturbed by the cries of babies nearest their own age, suggesting that they "speak the same language." We do not know how they could have learned to distinguish the special timbre and quality of this age group without experience.

The fact that babies are disturbed by the crying of other babies has prompted some researchers to conclude that empathy may be an inborn human quality.

## The Sense of Smell

Your baby may begin to sniff out the environment as soon as air hits the nasal cavity. Current research indicates that the sense of smell is not as highly developed in humans as hearing and vision. However, because this sense has important functions—warning of potential danger, helping in the search for food, adding to the pleasure of eating, even improving digestion—the ability to pick out odors is definitely part of your baby's repertoire at birth. This is clearly manifested by reactions you can readily observe—facial expressions, limb movements, changes in heart rate and respiration—as your baby avoids or is drawn toward certain odors.

The place where this olfactory sensitivity registers is a small area about the size of a postage stamp at the roof of each nostril. Mucus-covered tissue here contains a large number of receptor cells fringed with fine hairs pointing up into the air passageway through the nostrils. These fibers are actually branches of the nerve that carries messages upward to the underside of the brain. Also in the nose, endings of a different nerve respond directly to airborne substances, producing fast, painful sensations such as those brought on by a whiff of ammonia. This instant "smoke" alarm system protects both babies and parents.

In the womb your baby's nose begins to develop a profile around the sixth week and is well formed by the fifteenth. With this incredible instrument, your child will eventually be able to recognize several hundred odors. At birth your baby will display strong preferences without any practice or experience.

Jacob Steiner, who photographed newborns reacting to certain tastes, repeated the procedure to see how they reacted to odors presented on cotton swabs held under their nostrils. A panel of adults had selected from a large number of artificial odors those that corresponded to "fresh" and "rotten" smells. An artificial odor of rotten eggs and a concentrated fish odor were unanimously classified as offensive, while a diluted artificial butter aroma was considered "milky" and mildly pleasant, and banana, vanilla, chocolate, and strawberry were considered "enjoyable."

Infants just born, before their first exposure to any food, responded in Steiner's experiment with clear signs of aversion or satisfaction to different food odors. The facial response to pleasant odors was similar to the response to sweet tastes noted in the earlier taste experiment; the response to offensive odors was one of disgust similar to the response to bitter tastes. Even babies born with malformations of the cerebral cortex reacted as the others, indicating the early development of this sense.

Your baby quickly identifies your odor, and this information becomes one more connecting link with you. Experiments show that if used and unused breast pads are placed on either side of a baby's head, the baby will turn more often to the side of the *used* pads, indicating recognition by odor.

They can do this a few days after birth. With another few days of experience being near you, your baby can tell your used breast pads from those of other mothers.

If you breast-feed, the baby will quickly learn to distinguish your particular underarm odor. In an experiment with two-week-olds, the babies picked out their own mothers from others on the basis of her unique armpit "signature." Bottle-fed babies could not do so. This is an example of learning based on experience.

Your infant is also capable of recognizing specific odors in compounds. Experimenters have used various combinations of licorice, garlic, vinegar, and alcohol to test for this. Newborns were clearly able to tell the difference between pairs of smells presented at different times, and between single components of mixtures.

## Sight

Sight is probably the most important of all the ways your baby connects with you. After all those days of feeling, tasting, and hearing inside the womb, babies appear eager to look upon the faces of their mothers and fathers. Newborns have an uncanny ability to pick out their parents from others at birth, and they arrive in a naturally alert state that permits them to gaze deeply at mother or father for an hour or so before finally falling asleep.

Of all the senses, vision is the most complex and has received the most attention from researchers. Infant vision gets "better" with each improvement in the ingenuity and methodology of the researchers—something that can be said of research on all the senses. Only two decades ago, a pediatrics textbook taught that newborn vision included little more than sensitivity to light. We know now that babies are ready to use their eyes at birth. Vision in all its complexity may not be perfect, but it is well advanced and adequate for immediate needs. After all, newborns do not have to read traffic signs or microfilm; what they are prepared for is the sight of their parents.

Seeing involves the development and coordination of a number of body parts: the eye itself, the muscles that move and adjust the eye, specialized photoreceptors within the eye that are sensitive to light and color, the ocular nerve and its relay stations (brainstem and thalamus) en route to the vision area of the cerebral cortex. Perfect vision requires the cooperation of all parts of this amazing chain.

In comparison with the rest of your newborn's body, which will grow many times its size in due time, the eye will grow only two or three times in total volume, and all in a short two years. The retinal image of whatever your baby looks at will double as the retina reaches full adult size in the first year. That makes seeing much more efficient. Scientists are trying to evaluate the effects of many changes taking place during this period of rapid development. Many of your newborn's visual functions are close to adult level at birth.

In seeing, impulses from the eye are carried through the optic nerve to various parts of the brain where they are interpreted. The first parts of this system become distinct between seven and ten weeks after conception. Construction and growth continue in some parts for as long as two years after birth.

Your newborn's pupils begin to adapt immediately to light intensity. This is true for both premature and full-term infants. They blink and thrust their heads back when struck by too much light. Changes in light not only cause substantial change in pupil size but changes in heart and breathing rates as well. In tests in which infants were presented with paired combinations of panels differing in brightness, the infants seemed to prefer intermediate brightness levels.

Although research findings differ in regard to the newborn's ability to accommodate or focus on objects at various distances, under favorable conditions infants can discriminate fine details and may even show adultlike acuity. At intimate distances of a foot or two, the newborn is well focused. One authority compares newborn acuity to that of a domestic cat—not a bad rating.

Some tests show that a newborn can follow or track objects almost as well as adults taking the same test. Tests show that newborns are able to focus their eyes on stripes or dots moving across a 180-degree field. The two eyes are well coordinated and the ocular movements purposeful. Studying progress in vision in the first year, other investigators found that acuities at one month were much better than previously reported and that resolution was perfect by eight months. Using other methods, researchers have found that, under some conditions, infants focus well as early as one month, while marked improvements in focus may be expected in the first two or three months after birth.

Newborn babies are all eyes. When awake, they are always looking at something, eyes moving about every half-second. Continual scanning of the surroundings begins immediately after birth. Infrared cameras show that scanning practice continues even in the dark.

If you catch your newborn in a quiet alert state, you can see how well the eyes pursue a slow-moving target. By the fourth day after birth, head movement is added to your baby's eye movement to increase the range of pursuit sideways. Pursuit in the up-and-down dimension is harder, but pursuit of any kind demonstrates fine motor coordination. Constant correction of the eye muscles is demonstrated by your infant's ability to keep a moving object in the field of vision.

You may wonder if your newborn sees life in living color as you do. Scientists have worked hard to determine how soon infants develop color vision. After elaborate detective work, investigators think that newborns are making precocious use of the rods and cones necessary for color vision. Many experiments with one-, two-, and three-month-old infants show that their reactions to color are similar to adults. It appears that color is a universal "language" which your baby shares with you.

By four months of age, babies detect and classify colors the way adults do. This is revealed when they pick out a novel color in a familiar group and then follow that color to different shapes. Psychologists see this as evidence of concept formation. In essence, infants "know" that color is a classification scheme. This implies remarkable maturity of brain and neural resources.

Discovery of what your newborn prefers to look at has been aided by a simple technique developed by Robert Fantz of Case Western Reserve University. Fantz looked through a peephole at a newborn's eyes while the infant was looking at a visual target. By recording the length of time the target was reflected on the cornea, he could tell not only what was being looked at but how long the newborn looked at it—a measure of interest.

An early finding of Fantz's research was that from birth onward, infants could fix their gaze on certain forms and distinguish them from one another. In other words, infants begin immediately after birth to attend selectively to what is going on around them and "begin *acquiring knowledge* about the environment at the first look."

Given a choice of targets, newborns usually looked more at patterned than plain colored surfaces, at complex rather than simple patterns, at curved rather than straight lines, at color rather than black and white, at three-dimensional rather than two-dimensional objects, and at faces rather than other objects. All this suggests your newborn has an appetite for variety, complexity, color, and true-to-life angles and people.

Normal vision involves depth perception to locate objects at a distance, detect their motion or position, and determine their height relative to our own.

Newborns, if properly supported and free to move their

arms, reach out and grasp at objects. They are not yet very good at this because they need more practice in controlling their arm and hand muscles, but their efforts demonstrate interest, purpose, and depth perception.

In one experiment, Tom Bower at the University of Edinburgh moved a large sponge-rubber cube straight toward newborns. They responded with eye-widening, head retraction, and interposing hands between object and face—an intelligent defense. When Bower created an *illusory* object by means of Polaroid filters and goggles, newborns reached out and reacted with scowls when they could not make contact. Obviously they were using depth-perception skills but were tricked by the goggles. The infants looked mystified when thwarted in their plans and expectations. Bower concluded that many visual talents are innate rather than learned, although versatility in the use of these talents improves with practice in the first few months after birth.

Further proof of purposeful movement and depth perception comes from experiments in Uppsala, Sweden, by psychologist Claes von Hofsten. A spherical tuft of red, blue, and yellow yarn was suspended from a motor-driven rod. As the yarn swung in a circular path in front of the infants' eyes, TV monitors recorded movements of arms, hands, face, and eyes.

Newborns were clearly able to orient their eyes and hands toward the moving tuft of yarn. While they were doing so, most movements of the arms and hands were forward, indicating intent. When the babies fixated well on the moving yarn, their aim came closer. Cameras recorded the hands opening up in forward movement and slowing down when approaching the target.

If babies accidentally touched an unnoticed ball during random arm movements, their eyes immediately darted in that direction. Likewise, if the eye was first to make contact, the hand quickly joined in pursuit, showing instant coordination of eyes and hands.

Infants did not try to grasp the tuft of yarn but showed they were paying attention to it by reaching toward it and looking at it. The coordination of vision, movement, and touch, so well illustrated here, is not learned but pre-adapted. Thus, three-dimensional vision and hand-eye coordination join the list of abilities that your baby is ready to use at birth.

In exploring the senses separately, it is difficult not to be impressed by the way newborns ingeniously combine and integrate them, as in looking at the source of a sound, turning away from an odor, sucking faster to get a certain taste or sound, or reaching for something seen. This smooth coordination of all modes of sensory experience is dramatic evidence of your baby's integration of brain and senses at birth.

CHAPTER 3

# *Learning and Remembering*

$A$s long as it was believed that babies had neither well-developed brains nor senses, it was hard to take seriously claims that they could remember or learn. Parents who talked to babies in the womb could not hope to defend the practice rationally. Their behavior was interpreted kindly as slightly bizarre, an affliction of parenthood.

Things have changed. Today you may be asked why you are *not* talking to your preborn. Books and classes coach you on when to start and what to say. In psychology laboratories, decades of tests have shown that babies learn in all the classic ways we do. Proof of learning means proof of memory as well because learning requires memory.

If you look for signs of learning and memory in your baby, you will find many. You will see that your baby's eyes and ears are tuned to the environment with incredible interest. Sleepiness aside, your baby plunges into life with keen, integrated senses, adapting quickly to smells and sounds and demonstrating a positive appetite for experience.

Even when hungry, babies may interrupt eating to listen to interesting sounds. The discovery that babies would rather listen than eat was a surprise to psychologists who believed that hunger was one of the basic drives underlying human behavior. The triumph of curiosity over hunger tells us a lot about how mentally alert babies are.

Babies appear to enjoy learning and thrive on stimulation. Thanks to our new knowledge about the workings of the early coordination of body and brain, explaining such things is easier than it used to be.

We have seen in chapters 1 and 2 how soon the preborn begins to react sensitively (eight weeks) and when behavior looks organized (twelve weeks). Some of this very early behavior may be evidence of memory and learning. Particular exercise movements, seen at three months and onward through pregnancy, may be repeated from memory. The "ballet" roll, seen at six months of pregnancy, may be a well-rehearsed gymnastic attainment based on memory and learning. This type of memory is known as procedural (how-to) memory.

Thumb-sucking, seen in preborns by four and a half months, is perhaps first learned, then remembered and practiced by your prenate. Amniotic breathing habits, made slower or faster initially by the chronic intake of toxic chemicals, may be continued after birth when the chemicals themselves are no longer present—another example of learning in the womb.

In the heartbeat experiment by Lee Salk (chapter 2), perhaps the newborns' frightened reaction to a heart sound at 128 beats per minute represented a flashback to some prior experience. The heart rate of the preborn can double when mother is badly frightened. Perhaps the newborn remembers this and therefore is upset when it later hears the rapid heartbeat.

## Varieties of Memory in the Preborn

Memory before birth was revealed in the cryprints of Swedish preemies who had learned certain speech characteristics of their mothers. This evidence for memory and learning was dated at five months after conception. It indicates that your preborn listens carefully to your voice and learns certain characteristics of your speech, the proof of which can be seen in side-by-side voice spectrographs.

Your newborn may also remember music heard before birth. In *The Secret Life of Your Unborn Child,* Thomas Verny relates the story of conductor Boris Brott of the Hamilton, Ontario, Symphony. As a young man, Brott discovered he could play certain pieces sight unseen. In conducting a score for the first time, he said, the cello line would jump out at him; he knew how it went before turning the page. He traced this to the fact that his mother, a professional cellist, had practiced these pieces over and over during her pregnancy.

Lullabies you sing in pregnancy may have unusual power to calm your child after birth. Fathers who have identified themselves to the preborn by saying, "This is your father speaking . . ." have reported to me how riveting these words appear to be to the child when spoken after birth.

Remarkably, your newborn can learn words and tell one from another. Called semantic memory, this is one of several types of memory currently being investigated. Research psychologists in Boston asked mothers to repeat the unfamiliar words *tinder* and *beguile* ten times, six times a day for two weeks, starting a couple of weeks after birth.

At the end of training and after delays of up to forty-two hours, the infants showed clear signs of recognition through eye activity, head-turning, and raised eyebrows. During this testing period the babies recognized and responded to these odd words more than to their own names. Researchers concluded that it was the frequent and regular exposure of these words that led to success.

The same team found exciting evidence that newborns process speech the same way others do. With newborns only seventy-two hours old, they checked for word recognition by presenting words from the left and right and noting the pattern of head turns. The words used were *tinder* and *beagle,* one serving as the standard, repeated word and the other as a novel alternative. Newborns reacted to the familiar repeated word in the expected way, paying less and less attention. When the novel word was used, the infants recognized it. This pattern proves that they were retaining the repeated word in memory and comparing it to the novel word.

The preborn can also become familiar with stories before birth, a discovery made by psychologists Anthony De-Casper and Melanie Spence at the University of North Carolina. They asked pregnant mothers to read aloud *The Cat in the Hat,* a Dr. Seuss story, twice a day during the last six weeks of pregnancy. A few days after birth, the babies were given the opportunity to hear recordings of two stories, the familiar one and another Dr. Seuss story not heard before. Outfitted with earphones and a special nipple that let them change the story heard by sucking faster or slower, ten out of twelve newborns changed their speed of sucking to arrive at the familiar story.

This suggests that the babies heard and remembered the story, could tell the difference between stories, and "voted" for the one they knew already. We do not know, of course, just what they remembered or what the story meant to them. Could it be just pleasant words, sweet nothings?

A partial answer to this question comes from another study done with similar equipment by psychologists in Paris. The French newborns proved that they could pick out their own mother's voice from a field of other voices. They also showed a preference for their own mother's voice by sucking at whatever speed necessary to hear her voice—but only if she read normally. If the mother read words backward, the babies stopped listening. The mere sound of her voice was not enough.

## Importance of Memory

Without memory and learning, life cannot proceed safely. What if you lost your memory while driving on the freeway, or if you woke up in the morning forgetting how to spell? Experience is priceless, but without memory and learning it becomes worthless. Such a calamity is experienced in families where a member has been struck by brain disease. They may no longer recognize close relatives or remember what they have just been told. Carrying on a relationship with anyone means carrying forward some remembered history. Remembering your own history gives you a sense of self, an identity.

Fortunately for all of us, memory normally works well, and we can gain something from each new experience—that is, we learn. Sometimes we learn quickly, sometimes gradually, but sooner or later we catch on and adapt our behavior to what we remember.

How easily a baby can learn is seen in a simple experiment with two pacifiers. Newborns were first given a pacifier while blindfolded, limiting information to the sense of touch. One pacifier was normal, the other nubbly. Later, when shown the pacifiers, the babies looked longer at the particular one they had experienced earlier in their mouths. What the babies learned via touch was instantly available by sight.

When you hold your baby, the baby will mold itself to you and learn your contours. The secret to this is the integration of both inward and outward senses with memory. In a study at the University of Geneva in Switzerland, women were asked to pick up newborn babies in the dark, keeping absolutely silent. The babies made a more relaxed and complete postural adjustment when their own mothers picked them up—thus, in spite of the absence of visual and hearing cues, the babies recognized their own mothers. As noted in chapter 2, your breast-fed newborn will learn your unique breast and underarm odors in the first week.

In your first days together, your infant will be learning from you some of the difference between night and day. You need to be together for this to happen. A Boston group charted the amount of activity in the cribs of newborns who were rooming with other babies in a nursery and those who were rooming with their mothers. The babies kept with their mothers learned the difference between day and night and began adjusting wakefulness and sleep in just three days. The nursery babies had not learned it after eleven days.

Of course, you are not the only object of your baby's attention. When exposed to graphic designs of faces, double arrows, barbells, and stars, newborns are able to remember them. Four-day-old babies look more often at the novel design placed in a field of familiar designs. Even premature babies can distinguish novel color patterns from familiar ones.

## Discoveries about Learning

Many formal proofs of infant learning have come from experiments in psychology laboratories over many years, but not without trial and error. In retrospect, the first methods used to test for infant learning were more suited to animals or adults than to babies. Results were disappointing, and investigators sometimes reached false conclusions. Alleged deficits in the infants turned out to be deficits in the experimenters and their methods.

Critics now admit that the ability of infants to remember and learn has been grossly underestimated. Even the most popular type of experiment (in which one variable at a time is tested) is faulted because it does not take into account the natural complexity of newborns. The flexibility of the newborns themselves may account for the fact that we have been able to learn so much with experiments that were so limiting.

Infants have taught us a lot. They refuse to be handled like rats. If they get bored, they quit experiments. When drowsy or preoccupied, they do not bother with tests and consequently do not test well. What psychologists have learned can save you a lot of trouble in trying to help your baby learn. Here are four basic guidelines:

1. Communicate with them when they are fully awake and not already occupied (sometimes called the quiet alert state).
2. Use stimulations that are simple enough and slow enough to get the infant's attention.
3. Repeat things often enough.
4. Keep alert to signals of how well the baby is tolerating and integrating the experience.

Because infants cannot move their bodies or respond verbally as adults can, you have to figure out and use their natural communication system. In scientific studies this means paying sharp attention and finding something that can serve as a signal, some gesture or behavior that is already in the baby's repertoire that can be measured or recorded. Under these conditions, newborns demonstrate how well they pay attention and catch on. They do so well, in fact, that learning expert Lewis Lipsitt of Brown University said long ago that the newborn is "about as competent a learning organism as he can become."

What has been discovered may both thrill and horrify you: newborns seem to be learning all the time. In the laboratory, learning is given different names: classical conditioning, reinforcement conditioning, habituation, and imitation. Lurking behind each of these terms is something you can use to understand yourself and your children better.

The first scientific proof that infants were learning came from Russian psychologists experimenting with the process of classical conditioning pioneered by Ivan Pavlov. This is a process involving repetition and pairing of unrelated events. Following this system in 1948, American psychologist David Spelt taught preborns two months before birth to respond to the sound and feeling of a vibrator. While the vibrator was applied to the mother's abdomen for five seconds, a loud noise was made by a clapper hitting a box—a noise calculated to bring about a change of position in the womb. After many such pairings, the preborn learned to make this change in position in response to the vibrator alone.

One of the earliest American studies (1928) involved sounding a bell while pricking the sole of an infant's foot with a pin (something that would not be done today). Naturally the infants cried. After a dozen pairings, the sound of the bell by itself was sufficient to bring on the crying. In hospitals, babies' heels are routinely punctured to obtain blood samples. William Liley tells of babies in New Zealand who had to have as many as ten heel punctures in the first seventy-two hours after birth. For weeks and months afterward, he said, these babies would promptly cry and pull away if someone thoughtlessly grasped their foot. They remembered.

Among the processes that have been conditioned in infants are heart rate, pupillary dilation and constriction, eye blinks, sucking, and various reflexes. You can be watchful for accidental pairings of oft-repeated events with unpleasantness in your daily activities with the baby. For example, in families where fighting often occurs at bedtime or meals, eventually just going to bed or eating meals may bring on bad feelings. On the positive side, you can concentrate on good pairings (fun in the tub, happy holidays) that lead to happy associations.

You might experiment with conditioning using the Babkin reflex, where the baby's mouth opens wide as you press on its palms. To condition this reflex, researchers have moved the infant's arms from its sides up to its head just before pressing the palms. After a number of trials, the arm movement brings on the reflex with no pressing of the palms at all. Infants have also learned to produce the Babkin reflex in response to certain sounds.

Like all of us, infants learn more quickly when their behavior is followed closely by a clear consequence, good or bad. If behavior is followed by attention or some other reward, the behavior is expected to get stronger; if followed by something distinctly negative (punishment), the behavior is expected to get weaker or stop.

Many experiments with newborns show how quickly they figure out what to do to get what they want. In one of the most impressive studies illustrating this, one-day-old newborns mastered a complex set of circumstances related to head-turning. Experimenters built on the fact that infants usually turn their heads to the side where they are touched on the cheek. Normally, they will do this about 30 percent of the time. By making a sweet solution available when the baby turned its head, the rate was raised to 83 percent. Once established at that level, infants were taught to turn their heads to the left at the sound of a bell and right at the sound of a buzzer to obtain the sugar solution. Infants quickly learned the sweet taste of success.

The signals were then reversed and the reward given for turns in the opposite direction. Infants who had learned bell-left and buzzer-right now had to forget this and learn bell-right and buzzer-left in order to get the reward. A gradual shift in behavior took place, producing a reliable effect once again. Newborns mastered all these moves in thirty minutes. In other experiments, infants have learned to make head turns to obtain visual rewards—they are not just motivated by sweets.

A different type of test for learning is based on the predictable way we stop reacting if something is presented over and over again, like noises, lights, tastes, or odors. We pay attention at first, lose interest, and finally ignore it. This is an important form of adaptation that saves us from wasted effort and attention to things that are irrelevant.

Your infant will listen to the same sound for a while, but if it goes on too long, the baby will stop listening, a phenomenon called habituation. After a lapse of time, however, that sound will again draw a response (dishabituation). Habituation and dishabituation show that your baby can tell the difference between the familiar and the novel. Detecting these differences requires memory for what is old and perception of what is new—a significant integration of information. Therefore, this type of learning gives us another look at the mind of your newborn.

Newborn babies have demonstrated habituation and dishabituation in all five of the senses. Habituation to sounds can be tracked by changes in heartbeat. Babies show a declining heart rate with repeated presentations of the same sound. A change in tonal pattern will excite new interest and the heart rate will quickly increase. Before I knew about this, I used to hum in a funny way to entertain my babies. I'd bore them with something predictable and watch them get sluggish, then I would surprise them by changing tone and pace and watch them brighten. We both enjoyed it.

Because habituation is a normal brain response, it can serve as a diagnostic test. Traumatic birth impairs habituation. Some brain-damaged babies show no habituation at all; they just keep on reacting. Infants of mothers who received high doses of anesthetic in childbirth may require as many as four times more trials to habituate to a stimulus than those whose mothers received little anesthesia. This difference shows in tests of infants as long as a month after birth.

Your baby may be experiencing some form of habituation even before birth. A study showed that babies who spent their prenatal months living around the airport at Osaka, Japan, were not disturbed by loud overflights after delivery in a hospital under the flight path. Babies who came to that hospital from quieter places, however, were not prepared for all these airport noises. Half of these babies awoke screaming during overflights.

In your womb the baby listens to familiar and novel aspects of your humming and singing, the ambiance of your home, and the stories you read out loud. If you live in a noisy area, your baby will get used to noise—and perhaps wake up if it gets suspiciously quiet.

For decades, psychologists have appreciated how quickly young children copy behaviors they see around them. Imitation is one of the major ways we all learn. Until recently, however, child development experts were sure that babies were unable to learn by imitation until they were almost a year old. On theoretical grounds, it was declared impossible; when it happened, the experts said it must be something else.

Objections can still be heard in the psychological community, but experiments in several independent laboratories around the world show that newborns can indeed imitate. This display of infant brainpower is in a class by itself; it represents a paradoxical kind of learning—learning without tedious repetition (classical conditioning, habituation), without reward (reinforcement), and even without practice. It is a complex but innate mental ability.

If you catch your baby in the quiet alert state (not occupied otherwise) and stick out your tongue, you will probably see an exhibition of imitation. This was systematically studied by Andrew Meltzoff and Keith Moore of the University of Washington. They assembled a group of newborns, put them in a well-padded infant seat in a controlled environment, and showed them several gestures: sticking out the tongue, lip protrusion, wide-open mouth, and a sequential movement of the fingers.

Everything was videotaped, one camera zooming in on the faces of the infants and another trained on the face of the experimenter. Infants never saw the experimenter's face before testing. The responses obtained were then judged by a panel of observers who did not know which of four gestures had been shown. The infants were able to imitate all the gestures.

They were also able to remember a gesture and imitate it after a short delay. Investigators left a pacifier in the infant's mouth for two and a half minutes after presenting a gesture, effectively preventing immediate response. When the pacifier was removed, the infants proceeded to imitate the gesture they had seen two and a half minutes before. This demonstrates both memory and imitation. Meltzoff calls this an innate skill that enables a newborn to participate in social experiences from birth onward.

Newborns can also imitate meaningful emotional expressions. Adult expressions of happiness, sadness, and surprise were successfully imitated by newborns about thirty-six hours old in experiments by Tiffany Field and colleagues at the University of Miami. Expressions were accurately guessed by judges who could see only the babies' mouth, eyes, and brow. Reliability of these judgments was checked by split-screen videotaping where the infants' and adult models' expressions appeared side by side. Later experiments by this same group proved that premature newborns could do this, too. Field calls imitation "a very special skill."

## Joyful Learning

Those who have concentrated most on infant learning have discovered that learning is important, stimulating, and satisfying to infants. An early discovery involved crib mobiles. One group of infants was given mobiles they could control by moving a leg or an arm, while the other group had mobiles they could only watch passively. Infants who found out that their action could make the mobile move ended up smiling and cooing. The passive observers did not. It was not the mobile itself but the discovery of personal control that delighted the infants.

Two world leaders in infant studies, Hanus Papousek of Munich and Tom Bower of Edinburgh, say that babies express pleasure in learning. This does not mean that your baby will find learning all fun and no work. Papousek notes that infants go through a predictable sequence of emotions when they are working on a problem, just as adults do. On their faces you can see clear signs of puzzlement, confusion, displeasure, and satisfaction, depending on what stage of problem-solving they are in. Their facial expressions seem related to the success of their learning efforts.

Learning and problem-solving are mind games that give pleasure. When babies work out a solution to a problem or get control of something, they brighten up and break into smiles. Bower tells of a blind baby who had never been seen to smile. When the baby's legs were hitched to a mobile that made a sound when it moved, the baby quickly discovered he could activate the sound by kicking. That experience brought his first smile.

Bower notes that babies will quit working on experimental tasks in the psychology lab if they are too simple or repetitive. Once babies have mastered a particular task, they lose interest and withdraw attention until something new is introduced. To induce them to continue, psychologists must keep the tasks challenging but not too challenging.

You can make use of this principle with your baby. Successful education requires a comfortable balance. When tasks are too uncertain or too difficult, your baby's curiosity will turn to fear and distress. If the task is too simple, boredom may set in.

That babies learn just for the fun of it comes as a surprise to scientists. Accustomed to the way babies learned by tedious pairings, or by various reward incentives, they were amazed to find that babies went right on learning after the rewards had ceased. From this, scientists were persuaded that learning must be intrinsically rewarding, a treat in itself.

## Thriving on Stimulation

If you want to help your baby grow and develop to full potential, you will find encouragement and guidance from the new field of studies in infant stimulation.

Are you planning a home nursery for your baby? Not long ago this was considered the best possible treatment for infants—a room all to themselves. When parents left babies alone by the hour, they thought they were doing them a favor. After all, this was what hospitals did, and hospitals presumably knew what was best for babies. At that time no one thought babies were being deprived or held back in growth. Women in "civilized" countries felt sorry for mothers in "primitive" countries who had to carry their babies everywhere in a shawl. But these babies were lucky.

An abundance of research now points to the advantages of having more contact, not less, with newborns. Even small amounts of extra attention around the time of birth can make a significant difference in health, growth, and learning.

Stimulation can be offered in many forms, but the first and primary stimulation should be in the bosom of mother and family: keeping your newborn at your side after birth; holding, cuddling, and breast-feeding; exposure to music, color, things to see and touch; and a normal environment of adult activity and conversation. This is not a prescription for bedlam after birth but for normal interactions with peaceful parents.

Infants seem to welcome and thrive on stimulation, providing it is not overdone. When it is, your infant will send out distress signals, retreat, habituate, or just go to sleep. To determine the right balance, take your cue from the preferences your baby shows. The goal is not to force or overwhelm but to provide a variety of sensory experiences: movement, tasting, smelling, touching, seeing, and hearing. This approach of light mental and sensory "calisthenics" is exactly opposite from the institutional plan of infant isolation, quiet nurseries, and long hours of doing nothing.

Your baby's physical, emotional, and mental development can be enhanced measurably by extra attention and stimulation. Spending extra time with your baby seems to pay off handsomely. Pediatricians Marshall Klaus and John Kennell have reviewed seventeen experiments with this time variable alone. Infants who had as little as fifteen minutes with their mothers after birth, compared to those immediately taken off to a nursery, were found to smile more and cry less during observations three months later.

One study found that early contact of mother and baby resulted in more advanced language ability and higher intelligence. In this group of twenty-eight mothers, half were with their babies for one hour right after birth and for five hours a day for the next three days. The other half got only a glimpse of their infants after delivery, had brief contact in the next twelve hours, and a half-hour at feeding times. By the end of the first month, differences in the babies were already apparent. When tested again at two years and five years of age, children who had that extra early contact with their mothers scored consistently higher on IQ tests and showed better language comprehension, vocabulary, and expressive ability.

Your infant will be in a state of heightened alertness and responsiveness in the hours surrounding birth. If delivery is done without drugs, expect your baby to be wide-eyed and alert for an hour or more. This is a time for gazing at each other and engaging in other deeply personal communication. At this time, your baby's memory and learning ability seem to be enhanced. Researchers are not sure if the surprising effect of extra attention at birth is due to the extremely alert state of the newborn or to the effect of the baby on the mother. In either case, once mothers are really involved with their infants, all subsequent interactions are enriched.

Studies have shown that babies handled more tend to gain weight faster, grow taller, and develop motor coordination and muscle control sooner. When parents who had more early contact with their babies are observed with their children months and years later, they seem to show greater confidence, interest, and affection toward them. The babies show more trust, act more contented and secure, smile sooner and more frequently, and interact more personally with their mothers than do babies who missed this extra attention.

A critical need for stimulation is seen in premature and low-birth-weight infants. Ruth Rice, a nurse and psychologist, proved that a precise ritual of stroking and massage could help these babies catch up in their neurological development. In a Florida nursery full of preemies under four pounds, psychologist Tiffany Field organized a touching program that took fifteen minutes three times a day. The routine included stroking and caressing, sitting up, moving legs and arms, and a final massage—things any mother could do.

The effect of just ten days of this stimulation was extraordinary. The infants in the experimental touch group averaged 47 percent more weight gain per day on the same number of feedings and calories—metabolic magic. These infants were also awake more, were more active physically, showed better tolerance for distracting noises, were better able to calm and console themselves, and left the hospital six days earlier. When tested eight months later, "graduates" of the touching program were longer, heavier, had larger heads, and showed fewer signs of neurological problems than their counterparts in the same nursery who received standard care. With these results, it is no wonder that massage and physical activity, rather than isolation, are now recommended for all babies.

Motherpower can save babies in grave danger. In Bogotá, Colombia, four-pound babies (with a 50 percent chance of survival) were saved by the "kangaroo method." Instead of placing the preemies in incubators, pediatricians "packed" them head-up between their mother's breasts to be carried about. With mother's milk, heartbeat, voice, and constant activity going for them, rates of infection, illness, and death fell; nine out of ten lived.

An obvious tribute to the infant mind is the Infant Stimulation Education Association, founded by another nurse-psychologist, Susan Ludington of Los Angeles. The Institute offers comprehensive education in infant stimulation, including courses, bibliographies, and publications. Ludington's philosophy is that infants should be given a chance to reach their full potential and that stimulation to foster growth is their natural birthright.

In stimulating the vestibular sense (balance), the Institute suggests that babies like to be picked up and put down, rocked, and wheeled in strollers. They enjoy straight-line and rotary movements but not jolting or shaking motion, which may bruise brain tissue. Suggestions for tactile stimulation include stroking with materials like fur, velvet, wool, and satin while saying, "(Child's name), this is soft. Can you feel soft? How does it feel? Do you like soft? Soft is on the right side, and now it is on the left side. Soft is on your nose, on your chest, it's on your hand, and soft on your knee."

The Better Baby Institute in Philadelphia, founded by Dr. Glenn Doman, teaches mothers how to teach their children to read, do math, enhance their intelligence, and develop themselves physically. The Institute believes that the younger the children, the better they learn. It offers parents a wide variety of courses, books, and instructional materials in many languages and in many countries. Doman began his work with breakthroughs in helping parents of brain-injured children to accelerate their growth and learning.

If you want to start stimulating the mind of your baby before birth, guidance is available from The Prenatal University, a program organized by obstetrician Rene Van de Carr in Hayward, California. Manuals and tapes tell you how to involve your preborn in the "Kick Game" beginning in the fifth month. The invitation to kick at designated practice times teaches the preborn that action can become communication.

The second lesson starts with "Hi, this is Daddy," and introduces words including *pat, rub,* and *squeeze,* which are coupled with tactile stimuli. Music and a few letters of the alphabet, along with demonstrations of light, dark, warm, and cold are added gradually. Special consideration is given to words and experiences that will be used to communicate during labor and delivery; for example, "This is a squeeze," which will be used to explain a contraction.

A look at the first thousand "graduates" indicates that they cry less at delivery, often have their eyes open when sliding out of the birth canal, are more alert, are more easily calmed by patting, rubbing, or music, and have superior levels of physical functioning. After birth these babies seem to turn more quickly, talk earlier, act more independent, and can concentrate for longer periods of time.

An experiment with a control group (a similar group that did not experience the program) showed that this simple program of prenatal communication had a significant effect on mothers and fathers as well as the babies. Mothers in the program had more positive pregnancies, were more attached to their infants, understood the babies' responses better, felt the birth process was easier than expected, and had a lower rate of C-sections than mothers who missed the program.

Discovery that newborns are able to remember and learn, making full use of their physical senses and an obviously good brain, comes as a happy surprise. In the next chapters we will see how newborns put these abilities to use in expressing their individual personalities and engaging in communication with unexpected virtuosity.

## CHAPTER 4

# *The Engaging Personality*

*Y*ou will discover for yourself, as all parents eventually do, that all babies are not alike. Even in the womb, babies signal their preferences, react differently to danger, and go about their exercises with (or without) gusto. From the range of signals that reach you, you will develop a sense of the personality within.

In breath and heartbeat, you and your preborn are one. You share meals, space, laughter, and grief, all the while linked by the ceaseless flow of body chemistry. When you drink, baby drinks. When the baby has hiccups, you feel the rhythmic tremors. You will find yourself talking to your unborn baby, perhaps even using a name, covering topics from light to serious. When asked if they really believe there is a person inside who can follow this conversation, most parents become shy and apologetic. But they continue to talk to the preborn—if not on scientific grounds, then intuitively; if not publicly, then privately.

Until recently, science provided little encouragement to parents looking for signs of personality before or soon after birth. Now, as knowledge of womb life and newborn behavior steadily increases, evidence can be found for those distinctive individual patterns and qualities of behavior that define personality.

With the latest instruments, scientists have observed, recorded, tested, filmed, and analyzed how newborns use their senses, muscles, and minds. They actively reach out, explore, experiment, invent responses, and pursue interests. They are capable of self-direction, emotional expression, and establishing significant relationships. In making known when they are pleased or displeased, they exert enormous influence on those caring for them. By being responsive, they demonstrate that they are prepared for interaction.

## Early Signs of Personality

Signs of self-expression and self-regulation will first come to you from inside the womb, where your prenate is an active passenger, kicking and squirming, exercising at will, and constantly adjusting to your activities and moods. Over a period of weeks and months your baby is sure to react to different kinds of music, familiar voices, assaults on your person, accidents, holiday fireworks, and emotional thunderstorms. The reactions you feel are probably more than mechanical; they may be largely personal.

As noted in chapter 1, your baby may be a fitness enthusiast. Spying on preborns with ultrasound, we know how varied and spontaneous their activities are. It is the spontaneity that makes them a vehicle of self-expression. Beginning from ten to twelve weeks after conception, weighing but an ounce, the preborn practices at will, with verve and regularity. Fetal movements at this age are not mechanical-looking but graceful and fluid.

Every preborn shows individual features at the end of the third month. The muscles of the face are developing in a pattern determined by heredity so that facial expressions are already becoming similar to yours. The face is getting prettier, the vocal cords are completed, affording other avenues of expression.

Signs of personality in the preborn were first reported by New Zealand's pioneering fetologist, Sir William Liley. He portrayed the prenate as "very much in command of the pregnancy," guaranteeing success by producing certain hormones at the right time and inducing all manner of changes in maternal physiology to make mother a suitable host.

Through some hormonal wizardry, the preborn solves the homograft problem, the rejection faced by all unusual growths or transplanted organs. Prenates determine the duration of pregnancy, decide which way they will lie, and which way they will present in labor.

Among other signs of intelligent individuality observed in utero, Liley lists these: repeated and purposeful avoidance of pressure from outside on bony areas; violent response to needle punctures or injections of cold solutions into the womb; reactions to tickling; and definite taste preferences (some babies are suspicious of saccharine and swallow less, while others love it and swallow more). Babies may react with elevated heart rates to a flashing light applied to the mother's abdominal wall. They react to loud noises with a startle.

Researchers have observed a strange response to withdrawal of amniotic fluid after amniocentesis. In this procedure, which has become increasingly common, a needle penetrates the womb to withdraw a sample of fluid to verify possible genetic defects. Prenates about sixteen weeks from conception were filmed after needle puncture by doctors in Denmark. Half of them showed a striking, somewhat ominous reaction: they didn't move for two minutes.

Half of them also lost the variations normally found in a series of heartbeats. This flat, unvarying heartbeat pattern is also seen in very sick babies or babies who have been hit by a dose of Valium or some other drug. Because none of the fetuses showed this pattern before amniocentesis, researchers concluded they were reacting to the procedure itself. What we see here is not indifference, but a sensitive, perhaps shocked reaction to what has just happened in the sanctuary where they live.

## Sexuality

It stretches the imagination, but sonograms have shown surprising evidence for sexual feelings in the womb. The discovery was accidental, using one of the new generation of sonographs that make it possible to see even the smallest parts of the body. While looking for something else in a series of sonograms of a male fetus, doctors in New London, Connecticut, realized they were looking at development of an erection. Pursuing this unlikely finding, they eventually documented six such cases in males about twenty-six weeks from conception.

In the timetable of growth in the womb, male babies have a completed scrotum and penis by about sixteen weeks after conception. What these erections prove is that the appropriate nerve pathways are definitely working by twenty-six weeks, something not previously considered. We can speculate that these erections involve sexual feelings and are prompted by something sexual. In all six cases, the prenate was sucking his thumb during the erection.

Does sexual experience in the womb seem scandalous to you? Almost a hundred years ago, Vienna's Sigmund Freud shocked his colleagues (and parents of the world) by suggesting that infants and children had sexual feelings. He suffered considerable abuse for saying so. Sexuality in our children has a way of presenting itself before we are comfortable dealing with it. Ready or not, it appears that preborns are already sexual beings.

## Big Dreamers

Newborns sleep a lot. It's what they do most, typically sixteen hours a day for the first two weeks of life. But what you probably do not know is that fully half of that sleep time is spent *dreaming,* about eight hours in twenty-four. Premature babies (thirty weeks) dream 100 percent of their sleep time, which is most of the time. Nobody spends more time dreaming than newborns. This major discovery helps us to expand our concept of the infant mind and provides additional confirmation of personality before birth.

Dreams are a creative exercise of your baby's mind, a private, inward experience but not entirely secret. Dreams are electric, leaving a trail of brain waves and a telltale stream of nervous impulses to parts of the body that are active in the dream. It is only in the last quarter-century that sleeping and dreaming have been probed with the instruments of science.

The complexities of sleep are now studied with the aid of sensitive electrical instruments to measure brain-wave patterns, muscle activity, breathing, heart rate, and other vital signs. Studies reveal different stages of sleep occurring in cycles. One of these stages, identified as REM for rapid eye movements, is the dreaming stage. In non-REM sleep, in contrast, there is no movement of the eyeballs, and the whole physical system gets very quiet. Your newborn goes through several cycles of REM and non-REM sleep between feedings.

In the dream stage of sleep, brain and body are extremely busy, perhaps causing you to wonder if your baby is really asleep. Breathing speeds up and becomes irregular. Systolic blood pressure and production of certain steroids rise. Oxygen consumption increases, pressure rises in the brain cavity, males have erections, and the firing rate of single neurons of the brain may be as high as during the waking state. You can see large body movement and often a change in position. Your baby's brain, like the heart, kidneys, and other organs, does not rest in sleep but is very active indeed.

What we know about the sleeping and dreaming of newborns is largely from a study of newborns and premature babies by specialists at Columbia and Stanford universities. Using modern instrumentation, they found that babies start dreaming soon after falling asleep. If you watch babies go to sleep, you will observe this. (Adults, in contrast, begin with quiet sleep and dream later.)

An unexpected discovery was that the younger the newborns were in conceptual age, the more they dreamed. From 100 percent of sleep time at thirty weeks, dream time falls steadily to about 50 percent at forty weeks (full term). Then it falls consistently throughout life, to 20 percent of sleep time in the teens and 13 percent in old age.

Why is dreaming so important to babies? The authors of this research speculate that the impulses arising in the brainstem during REM sleep may somehow facilitate the growth and myelination of key sensory and motor areas of the nervous system. Non-REM sleep, in contrast, seems to promote integration and control in the hemispheres of the upper brain (cerebral cortex). In other words, dreaming is a brain exercise.

Your baby's dreams also have content, and the content may be serious. Breathing irregularities typical in REM sleep cause wide fluctuations in chest expansion and periods of no breathing at all for ten seconds at a time. If you are watching, this can be alarming. In adult sleep, such events are linked to what is happening in the dream, like talking, choking, laughing, and running. In dreams the full world of experience can be duplicated. Presumably, infant dreams are like this, too. In dreams, infants appear to be dealing with compelling events going on inside their own minds.

Watching fourteen newborns dreaming, researchers noted many signs of consciousness: grimaces, whimpers, smiles, twitches of the face and extremities, and shifting of body and limbs. There were frequent ten- to fifteen-second episodes of writhing of torso and disturbances of limbs, fingers, and toes ("bad" dreams). They saw on the babies' faces what they felt were expressions of perplexity, disdain, skepticism, and other signs of emotion and thought.

Apparently, some dreams are boisterously amusing. One mother told me that her child laughed outright in dreams repeatedly during the first three months after birth.

While it is difficult to prove that newborn dreams are the same as adults' dreams, they appear the same in every measurable way. The authors of this study point out that because dream activity is associated with a segment of the brainstem that develops early, there is no reason why dreams cannot occur early in gestation and cannot contain material from the baby's experience to date. There is also no reason to doubt that when your baby smiles in dreams, it is a sign of pleasure.

## A Collection of Smiles

Smiling is one of the most engaging and rewarding expressions of infant personality, but experts used to think it was impossible in newborns. That helps to explain why newborn smiles are still a well-kept secret. Newborns can and do smile. Watch for them.

Actually, since the discovery of dreaming in preemies, we have had evidence of smiling a couple of months before full-term birth. Since premature babies dream most, they also smile most. I can't help wondering what they are dreaming about, especially when they are smiling.

Your baby *can* smile at birth—a rare but important phenomenon, especially to you. Pediatricians used to say smiles were nothing but gas, but since the work of French obstetrician Frederick Leboyer and the increase of gentle birthing practices, more babies have been seen smiling at birth. Some of them smile when given a warm bath by their fathers.

Babies born underwater may hold the record for smiling at birth. One father reported after an underwater birth that his daughter smiled blissfully for several minutes. Can you accept that these smiles (or piercing cries, as the case may be) indicate how babies actually feel about their birth?

You never know when or how often your baby is going to smile. Harvard pediatrician Peter Wolff observed a group of four newborns intensively for five days. He found wide variations in the frequency of smiling, from six to sixty-eight smiles per baby, mostly counted in the dream state. A few smiles were associated with stooling or urination, a sign of some pleasure, no doubt. Twin girls in the study were the biggest smilers; they smiled six and ten times more, respectively, than the other two in the study—clear evidence of a difference in personality.

Technical studies show that early smiles are partial smiles involving mouth and cheeks but not the muscles up as high as the eyes and forehead. This does not mean they are necessarily inferior or insincere; they could reflect a lack of muscle development as well as a lack of enthusiasm. Full, deliberate, and controllable smiles seem to appear with predictability at forty-six weeks from conception (six weeks after a full-term birth). This smile has been dubbed the social smile because it comes in reaction to a social greeting. Baby experts have called it the first "real" smile; this is a scientific put-down. In my opinion, we are overdue in accepting *all* infant smiles as meaningful and each smile as a legitimate part of the total smiling repertoire.

As your baby gets older, smiling becomes a more frequent expression of personality. You have a lot to do with encouraging (or discouraging) smiles, as an experiment by psychologist Yvonne Brackbill revealed. In a group of four-month-old babies, half were picked up and smiled back at whenever they smiled. The smiles of the other half were ignored. Smilers who were encouraged greatly increased their rates of smiling compared with those ignored.

Having discovered this, the experimenters switched from encouragement to discouragement with the smilers. During the initial part of the experiment, babies gazed with rapt attention at faces smiling back; when the experimenters quit smiling back, the smiling rates plummeted. After encountering a series of blank faces, the babies would not even look at the experimenter's face. They turned their heads and eyes away!

As smiles were rejected, relationships collapsed. To keep the babies from turning away, their heads were propped up with rolled blankets. Unable to turn their heads, babies turned their eyes to the ceiling; they refused to exchange glances. This experiment is dramatic proof that when a baby smiles, it is a very personal message of vital importance. Motherpower is also clearly illustrated here. If you want a smiling baby, you know what to do.

High-tech analysis of infant smiles later in the first year reveals that smiles are more expressive than had been thought, and in ways we cannot see with the naked eye. Study of facial movement and brain activity reveals that babies actually give more generous smiles to their mothers than to strangers. The big smiles reserved for mother involve more muscles and activate the right frontal region of the brain, while smiles given to strangers activate fewer facial muscles and the left side of the brain. Whatever the meaning of this curious difference, these measurements prove that babies are feeling and expressing different things in their smiles. If you thought your baby had a special smile just for you, you were right.

## Close Encounters

Your baby's personality comes through in close encounters that are impressively personal. Rare film and video footage, slowed down for a careful look, show engrossed attention and synchrony of movement between newborns and their parents. An example is the amazing encounter between a newborn and his father captured on film by Daniel Stern of Cornell University Medical College.

The baby, arriving home from the hospital after birth, is held in his father's arms. Run in slow motion, the film shows that as the father's head begins to move down, the baby's head begins to move up to meet him. This happens several times. When the father's right hand begins to move up from his side, the baby's left arm, which had been hanging over the opposite side, begins to move up at the same time. The opposite hands of father and baby then come together over the baby's middle, where the baby clasps his father's little finger and at that moment falls asleep.

This choreography, for which the father has had lots of muscle practice and the baby none, involves exquisite visual perception, anticipation of action, desire to participate, and muscle synchrony of head, arms, and hands. What looks so casual is a brilliant achievement for the newborn as father and son meet and embrace. In reporting this, psychiatrist Louis Sander comments, "It boggles the mind as to how synchrony of this sort can exist."

Synchrony is just one of the words that describe how newborns establish firm contact with mothers and fathers. Bonding and attachment are more common terms for this closeness. Scientists further describe the relationship of parent and child as interlocking, or reciprocal. All these terms recognize that your newborn is capable of intimate engagement, self-assertion, and, to the limit of its strength, even companionship and entertainment.

As an interested mother you can watch for those special quiet alert states and make the most of them by looking face-to-face, smiling, talking, singing, cuddling, and kissing. These intimacies, for which the infant is definitely prepared, may well be the foundation for interactive play, love, and lovemaking in later life. In a favorable environment of closeness and appreciation, the baby's personality will bloom.

## Face to Face

In your baby's face you will see those individual qualities and patterns that constitute personality. Faces are the natural meeting place for mutual discovery and friendly exchange. What has been so well hidden, until exposed by modern research, is the incredible ability of the newborn to see in *your* face the qualities of *your* personality.

Many studies show the special fascination babies have for faces. Infants only nine minutes old, with no prior visual experience, will single out normal-looking faces in a parade of facelike designs. They will turn their eyes and heads to follow blank faces and faces with the eyes, nose, and mouth in the wrong locations as well as normal-looking faces, but they will give significantly greater attention to the normal faces. Having never seen one, how do they know which of the designs is closer to the real thing?

Just as hard to explain is how your newborn baby can pick you out in a gallery of "mug shots." Within three or four minutes of birth, babies presented with big photos of women, or faces looking out of portholes, will find and look at their own mothers. Your baby "knows" which one you are. How can this be done without previous experience?

When faces are not right—especially yours—your baby can become alarmed. This reaction is very personal; it is also proof that your baby remembers you from before and is troubled by the change.

In Boston a group of new mothers were asked to wear masks and remain silent during one feeding on the seventh day after delivery. One of the masks was flesh-colored, had two eyeholes, and covered the face to the hairline. The other mask was white gauze draped from a green surgical cap. Each baby saw his or her mother in both masks at different times.

Clearly, the babies didn't like what they saw. Visibly

upset, they changed positions and looked away from their mothers. After seeing the flesh mask, babies in their cribs increased their surveillance of the environment as if they were anxiously checking for other strange developments. They went to sleep more rapidly, as if escaping into a more pleasant world. After both masks, babies took less milk, were fussier, and cried more.

One mother, describing her baby's reaction to the flesh mask, said, "she kept looking and looking at me like she couldn't believe it . . . she was very upset . . . and spit up for the first time." After the gauze mask, this baby didn't want to have anything to do with her mother; "she peeked, and that was it."

All babies in this study were rooming-in with their mothers and had had six days of normal breast-feeding before the masks appeared. When the experiment was repeated with nursery babies, the reactions were much less and sleep was unchanged. Apparently the nursery babies didn't know their mothers that well and hadn't begun to care. This indicates how rapidly your relationship develops when you are together. In reading your facial expressions, your baby will quickly form impressions, develop expectations, and begin caring about you. Two personality profiles are developing, yours and your baby's.

## Voice Link

Your baby hears your voice long before birth, of course, and this link with you is expanded after birth. Tests after birth show the personal dimensions of this bond—your baby is especially attracted to *your* voice.

Working with newborns in France and the United States, psychologist Anthony DeCasper and his colleagues made it possible for infants to hear various sounds and voices as they sucked at different speeds on a nipple. Among the possibilities were recordings of their own mother reading

"To Think That I Saw It on Mulberry Street!" by Dr. Seuss and another woman reading the same story. Measuring pauses in sucking bursts by the second, they discovered that the babies would suck at whatever speed was needed to get the sound of their mothers reading the story—they preferred her voice. The two-day-olds in DeCasper's study had no trouble identifying the voices of their mothers, whether they spoke in English or French, from other women and men.

To do this, newborns had to be capable of understanding speech rhythmicity, intonation, frequency variation, and phonetics. Memory experts would note that they had to hold their mother's voice in memory while comparing it with the novel voice.

When given a choice between male and female voices, babies generally choose the female voice, perhaps because that is what their ears are best equipped to hear. They can identify their father's voice, but if they have to choose between that and a heartbeat sound, they prefer the heartbeat, perhaps because it is a more intimate friend. (Fathers should not take this too personally; they just can't be around as much as the heartbeat or the mother's voice. Besides, no studies have been made of fathers who have been *actively* in communication with their babies before birth.)

Voice games make a fine vehicle for the expression and interaction of personalities. Any interested parties can play by shifting up to a higher pitch, "duetting" any vocal sounds the baby happens to make, mixing in some light tickling perhaps, and exaggerating facial expressions. If you are in a mood to express your own personality, try peek-a-boo games, nursery rhymes, silly imitations, and other "sweet nothings."

Remarkably, your infant is ready to either follow or lead in these look-and-sound games. Motion pictures synchronized with sound recordings of infants and parents reveal that infants are leading the play about 90 percent of the time. This means that the parents were extremely attentive and allowed the infants to take the initiative. By being responsive in this way, you make room for the personality of your newborn to take center stage.

Typically, your baby will start things off by making a favorite sound. As an interested parent you imitate it a few times. After a respectful pause the baby contributes another noise, something in the current repertoire, capped off on occasion with a cheerful vowel-like sound or a joyful squeal. In this intimate and rewarding dialog, together you show off your engaging personalities, one individual reaching out to another.

## CHAPTER 5

# A Gifted Communicator

*I*nfants, as a group, make plenty of noise, but until recently their noise was not considered intelligent. Infants have always talked with their bodies, turning red with rage, tensing with fear, clenching fists emphatically, but too often we have been unmoved by their messages. Newborns have been talking to a wall.

While we have been earning low grades in receiving their messages, the latest scientific research indicates they have been doing superbly well receiving ours. Infants scrutinize adult faces and moods and react accordingly. Looking and listening with amazing precision, they wait for us to join them in intimate dialog. Newborn communication is quick, sometimes instant. This ability is so precocious, it may be inborn rather than learned.

## Communication Before Birth

Your own first communications to your unborn child probably begin without awareness or intention in the sounds of music, your heartbeat, the din of unusual commotion, and your humming, singing, talking voice. The preborn within is alert and eavesdropping.

One of the earliest hints of attentive fetal listening can be seen in intrauterine photos of a prenate, eyes sealed but looking profoundly absorbed, delicately holding the umbilical cord. This cord links the solitary womb with the surrounding world.

Better than a television cable, the umbilical cord pulses with the traffic of life passing back and forth between you and your unborn. Ever-present, it is a handy plaything but alive, changing, and flooded with information. This lively conduit may be a biofeedback unit from which the baby gains information about the flow of nutrients and the slowing or speeding of circulation, a type of maternal-fetal monitor that carries reassuring or worrisome news.

**Touch-Tone Equipment.** I can't believe the fetus is oblivious to the life-and-death messages passing through the cord. My speculation is that some kind of intelligence is gained through a combination of touch and hearing. Touch is a well-developed sense, highly visible after birth in constant touching, mouthing, tasting, grasping, poking, and shaking things. Think of this massive touching activity as two-way communication: bringing information in (how does it taste, feel, sound?) and sending it out (I like that and want more).

Touching is a basic means of communication for all of us, supplying a steady stream of information from shaking hands, hugging, holding, and feeling. Think how much you touch as you shop, for example. (We touch so automatically that signs have to warn us not to.)

Your preborn has hands and fingers by the seventh week of pregnancy. By the fourteenth week, the preborn can bring its hands together and may start thumb-sucking. Exploring, touching, and grasping are inevitable. Using their ingenuity, preborns may be like those prisoners of war who kept in touch with each other by attending to vibrations in the water pipes.

The auditory network that feeds data into the touch system is also busy scanning the atmosphere for broadcasts of your voice. Speech lessons definitely begin before birth. One of the pioneers who discovered this, Henry Truby of the University of Miami Medical School, told me in a personal conversation (1983) that spectrographs of the newborn's voice would reveal if it was a first child, had been a problem pregnancy, or had endured marital conflict in utero. All these, he said, would be reflected in the child's voice and be communicated in speech in later life. You may not be paying much attention to your prenate, but your prenate is paying close attention to you.

**Speaker Phone.** It has been known for centuries that babies can cry in the womb, but it is little taught and seems a well-kept secret.

Crying in the womb is possible whenever air gains access to the amniotic cavity and the fetal larynx—as happens in rupture of membranes or passing a catheter through the cervix. Before the days of sonograms (images made by recording high-frequency sound waves bouncing off the fetus), when obstetricians used to do air amniograms, they had to caution mothers to stay in an upright position for several hours after the procedure so that air would be kept away from the fetal larynx; otherwise they could have the unsettling experience of hearing the fetus cry.

Robert Goodlin, chief of perinatal medicine at the University of Nebraska Medical Center, tells us that if there were air in the womb, the fetus could be heard crying much of the time. We have to presume that these cries are communicative and meaningful. Studies show that cries in the hours just before birth are caused by obstetrical maneuvers.

## Universal Languages

Newborns are famous the world over for their sounds. During the first twenty-four hours the baby may create a symphony of noises: screams, whimpers, whistles, and whines, also coughs, burps, sneezes, hiccups, and grunts. On rare occasions you may hear pleasurable cooing, humming, or even laughs. All sounds carry information and are potentially useful.

Music and color are international languages that speak to

babies as well as adults in every culture. Similarly, crying is understood everywhere on Earth. Babies master this language long before birth. Body talk is spoken in all countries. Hand movements, facial expressions, and gestures have a compelling grammar of their own. Babies actively use this means of communication. Finally, emotions are another universal language requiring no translation. Emotion is a native language of the whole human race, and babies know it as well as adults.

**Newborn Cries.** Some babies arrive quietly, making little more than a gasp; they kick and wave vigorously and scan the horizon for mother. If the environment is peaceful, your baby may remain quietly alert, eyes bright and open wide for an hour or more after delivery. During this time, you will be moved by penetrating, intimate eye-to-eye contact. You will know you are communicating with each other. First looks like this help to forge strong family bonds between all who participate, including siblings.

As is legendary, most babies cry at birth, and lustily so. This cry has an imperative, provocative effect on almost anyone in earshot. Doctors and parents are prone to laugh nervously at these cries and say they are a sign of health and strength. This is a cruel joke. A baby's cry at birth is a distress signal and plea for help.

Not long ago, authorities taught that baby cries were random, simple, and undifferentiated sounds and therefore without meaning. This betrayed arrogance as well as ignorance. Since the invention of spectrography and other methods of recording sound, precise measurements have revealed what parents and grandparents have instinctively known, that cry sounds have definite meaning and character. Mothers have always learned to interpret baby cries and to tell their own infant's cry from another's.

Recordings show that cries are clearly different. There are specific cries for birth, hunger, pleasure, and pain. When these cries were played to hundreds of adults of all ages, including married and unmarried men, researchers found that nearly everyone could identify which was which.

Since this definitive work on the infant cry about a quarter-century ago, doctors have discovered that cries contain information about illness, malformations, malnutrition, and other growth problems. Cries of infants with chronic distress tend to be high-pitched and unpleasant.

All this underscores the fact that cries are a serious form of communication—if anybody is truly listening. *When* babies cry, *how* they cry, and *how much* they cry are indications of need, dissatisfaction, or distress. You may not be able to figure out all cries instantly, but if you know that your baby is trying to say something, you will get the message sooner or later.

Crying certainly is not a happy expression; it is like a strong "no" vote for whatever is happening. If we want to know what babies think about something, we could just listen to their cries. An example of this is crying when the umbilical cord is cut at delivery. In his crusade for birth without violence, Dr. Frederick Leboyer has suggested that the cord need not be cut at the moment of delivery but should be allowed to stop pulsing naturally. Some doctors disagree. But, judging from their cries, babies take a clear stand with Leboyer. They cry more frequently after cords are cut early, less when cords are cut late.

**Baby Body Talk.** Babies talk with the whole body. They express pain and contentment physically and totally. As noted earlier in connection with the senses, facial expressions quickly and accurately express your baby's reaction to various pleasant and unpleasant tastes and odors. Grimaces and frowns will eloquently convey your baby's reactions to light and sound. Complaints about the temperature will be unmistakable.

Newborns can already communicate with their hands. If

they grasp and hold on to your finger, it will tell you something. If you grasp and hold on to your baby's hand, won't *you* be saying something? Babies swing their arms around, obviously not yet in control of their fine muscles but expressing an exuberant interest in things. Hands are sent out like explorers to bring things back. They also serve as pointers telling you there is a target out there of interest to your baby.

Some hand positions are like a sign language that can alert you to the state the baby is in. The hands can tell us about degrees of consciousness from sleep to full alertness. Doctors Hanus and Mechthild Papousek have sketched five of these positions (see Figure 5-1). (You should have no trouble interpreting the negative feelings displayed by the closed fist.)

Body talk is communicative long before it is fully developed and under control. If you are open to this concept, you will be able to "talk" to your baby sooner than expected. One of the pioneering researchers who appreciated baby body talk was University of Edinburgh child psychologist Colwyn Trevarthen. Trevarthen saw the value of the awkward movements that come before smooth movements. Looking movements, he noted, are practiced before there is full efficiency in seeing; handling and reaching movements appear before the ability to easily grasp and manipulate objects; and speaking movements come long before a baby can "say" anything. What is important is that they express the baby's interests, intentions, and purposes. They tell us that something is on the baby's mind.

At times, your baby's body language can be unbelievably specific. This surprised researchers at Harvard University's Center for Cognitive Studies who filmed infants interacting with their parents over many weeks after birth. At times they introduced a three-inch toy monkey.

After viewing films of the infants, investigators realized that the babies moved differently when they were looking

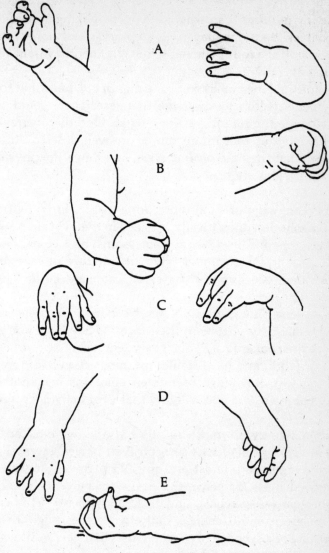

Figure 5-1. The Meaning of Infant Hand Signals
A=alert waking state; B=closed fists in uncomfortable or distressing situations; C=passive waking state; D=transitional states to sleep; E=sleep. By Hanus and Mechthild Papousek. *(Used with permission of the doctors Papousek and Academic Press.)*

at the toy monkey than when they were looking at parents. The babies' body language was so precise, researchers had only to look at a toe or a finger to tell whether the infant was looking at a toy or a person.

By the time the babies were one month old, hand and foot movements were so expressive that researchers could tell which *parent* the infant was looking at. Odd discoveries of this kind tell us that infant minds are well ordered, know who or what they are dealing with, and move the physical body appropriately.

**The Language of Emotion.**   Some babies arrive with a burst of emotion dramatically revealed in their vocal sounds, flailing arms and legs, facial expressions, and color. How could anyone fail to understand this mixture of rage and pain? Other babies appear contented, calm, and curious just after birth.

Newborns, like the rest of us, have inner feelings that become instantly visible on their faces. (They have not yet learned the "poker face.") Such expressions can be found all over the world and have similar meanings even in different cultures. The full range of human emotions may not be present at birth, but you will find that your baby does quite well.

When twenty-six mothers of newborns were asked to keep a record of emotions seen on their babies' faces, they reported signs of interest and joy (95 percent), anger (78 percent), distress (65 percent), surprise (68 percent), sadness and disgust (40 percent), and fear (35 percent). This is a worthy spectrum of feelings. Only twenty years ago it was something of a surprise to psychologists that newborns were capable of any specific emotions.

Videotaped in the first week of life, newborns show a range of emotions from pleasure to rage. Babies can go from sleeping to loud screaming in just thirty seconds. After studying many such records, one researcher concluded that if some babies were not swaddled and could free their hands, they would hit at whatever or whoever was nearest. Others have concluded that infants respond more globally and intensely to provocative circumstances than older people do. They are not at all shy about their feelings.

Acoustical analyses of infant voices show a continuum from maximal pleasure (laughter and squeals) to partial pleasure, emotional neutrality, partial displeasure, and maximal displeasure (a full cry). You can observe these emotional outbursts by their variations in pitch (low-high), duration (short-long), or loudness (decibels). The maximal displeasure signal is the loudest at over 2000 hertz. This is hard to miss. More to be cherished are the melodic contours of "partial pleasure" sounds—typically smooth, continuous, and relaxed, like cooing. This documentation of emotion was done with two-month-old babies by Doctors Hanus and Mechthild Papousek of the Max Planck Institute of Psychiatry in Munich.

## Ready for Dialog

You will be surprised, as many scientists were, to discover that babies are ready for dialog. As late as 1975, experts in developmental psychology were saying it was "doubtful at best" whether infants could recognize their mothers' voices or react to anything more than specific segments of speech sound. That was the year that spectrographs were pressed into service to understand the infant cry. The resulting cry-prints showed that even very immature preborns had already learned certain speech features of their mothers.

We know now that newborns listen with extraordinary precision to adult speech and to the crying of other babies. They also peer out at the world with incredible perception and quickly learn and respond to what they see. They even seem to read lips.

**Precise Listening.** An interesting example of precision listening comes from the 1978 French experiment cited in chapter 3 that indicated that babies would listen to their mothers read forward but not backward.

If babies can't understand words, why should they care what order the words are in? Researchers thought it might be the monotony of the voice when reading in reverse that caused the babies to lose interest. But isn't any story rather monotonous if it's in a language you don't understand? Do babies have a way of recognizing that backward reading is a form of nonsense? Whatever the reason, their listening is extremely precise.

Your infant will probably give curious attention to a variety of sounds. Psychologists videotaped babies a few days old responding to two speechlike sounds and two narrow-band noises coming from an overhead speaker. They were surprised at the mature quality of the responses to these rather strange sounds. Listening was judged by directional head movements, tongue-thrusting, and active mouth movements indicating involvement in what was going on. Attention also showed in eye-fixation, pupil dilation, visual search, and breath-holding. Some babies listened so intently they lifted their heads clear off the beds and maintained vigilance for three to five minutes at a time.

It's no secret that small children learn languages easily, but it is a surprise to scientists that babies share this special talent. Your baby will be able to detect differences in the smallest units of speech (phonemes), like "pa" and "ba." Babies are actually better at this than adults for the entire first year of life. Researchers found this out by exposing infants, at different months of the first year, to sounds of non-native languages. Compared with adults listening to the same sounds, the infants did better at recognizing the smallest differences, something they demonstrated by turning their heads toward new sounds within 4.5 seconds.

This talent was strongest during the first six months, then began to diminish gradually so that by one year of age, the infants were on the same level of ability as adults. What this means to you is that you can speak normally to your baby. You might speak slowly, distinctly, and raise the pitch, but your baby is better prepared than anyone else to listen to language.

Your newborn will be a discriminating listener to various kinds of cry sounds. Given a choice of white noise (a nondescript electronic background noise), computer-synthesized cries, and real cries, babies respond to real cries more. Among real cries, newborns respond most to babies in their own age group, less to babies five weeks old, and least to babies five months old. The cries of a baby chimpanzee were ignored.

The strongest reaction of newborns is reserved for recorded sounds of their own cries. Listening to themselves caused their normal heart rate to jump 7.5 beats per minute. Ordinarily, newborns cry in response to the wailing of other newborns, but they are less likely to start crying when they hear their own cries. If already crying, they are likely to stop when they hear their own cry. This means they have self-awareness.

Your quiet, alert newborn may also listen with incredible involvement to your speech. In 1973 psychologists at Boston University studied infants' bodily reactions to adult speech. Cameras were pointed simultaneously at the baby's head, eyes, elbows, shoulders, hips, and feet. A time-motion analyzer made it possible to study specific movements frame by frame, one second at a time. For example, arm movements could be scanned to locate the exact frame in which any change of direction occurred.

Adult speech was measured down to the syllable. Split-second analysis of these events revealed that babies in the first day of life were moving their bodies in synchrony with adult speech—a kind of entrainment or dancelike movement. All sixteen newborns in the study did this. They managed to sustain entrainment through speeches up to 125 words in length.

The same extraordinary listening occurred whether the speech was live or tape-recorded. Infants, already in motion when an adult began to speak, stopped whatever they were doing and moved in rhythm with the speech. They did not respond in this entranced way to recordings of disconnected vowels or to mere tapping sounds.

Infants come into the world prepared with precise listening skills to lock into human speech, especially of their mothers and fathers, and be totally involved.

**Perceptive Looking.**   Your baby arrives looking as well as listening. When awake, the baby's eyes are ceaselessly at work scanning everything in sight. This visual busyness is remarkably intelligent and selective.

The method devised by psychologist Robert Fantz of looking at the cornea of an infant's eye while the infant was looking at various visual presentations (see chapter 2) revealed that infants had preferences, could identify forms, and work with patterns. Before Fantz, the traditional view was that the visual world of newborns was initially formless and chaotic, and that they had to learn to see configurations. Fantz showed that form perception and pattern selection were innate rather than learned and that the highest level of the visual system, the striate cortex region of the brain, was already in service at birth.

An example of how your newborn makes use of these visual gifts is in treating toys as toys and people as people. In the films made at Harvard University mentioned earlier, infants reacted very differently in looking at their mothers and at a toy monkey.

Infants watched mothers with intense concentration in brief glances. As the mothers responded to them, the babies looked away and changed their gestures and sounds. Look-

ing at mothers followed a cyclic pattern of looking and looking away, four or five times a minute. Babies acted shy,
intensely interested but trying not to stare.

Looking at the toy monkey was exactly opposite. By three
weeks of age, infants stared wide-eyed at the toy for long
periods, hunched as if ready to pounce. Fingers and toes
were aimed at the monkey, and the baby's tongue kept
darting out toward it. Their bodies seemed immobilized,
faces serious, and eyes blinked only occasionally. No shy-
ness needed here.

In the same films it was obvious that babies knew when
their mothers were looking at them. Cameras were arranged
to show the faces of mother and infant side by side to reveal
exact timing of their interactions. When mothers were smiling and watching, the babies were inspired to perform large
limb movements and to vocalize.

Babies a few weeks old have an uncanny ability to recognize when facial movement fits with sound—a form of lip
reading. A typical experiment in this field might present a
split-screen choice of two faces speaking, accompanied by
one correct sound track. The babies look more at the face
that matches what they are hearing. They know which faces
and voices belong together—in any language.

Your baby expects to hear *your* voice when looking at you
talking. If the sound is someone else, it is very disturbing!
Likewise, if your voice is presented with someone else's face,
the baby senses something is wrong and turns away.

Older infants can match up happy and sad sound tracks
correctly with faces giving a sad or happy monolog, indicating knowledge of what emotional states sound and look like.

In an experiment with babies in London, nursery rhymes
were presented with normal facial movements half the time
and with a slight out-of-synch delay the other half. Even
though the delay between lips and sound was only 400
milliseconds, babies lost interest. They looked away significantly more when the sound was out of synch. This has led

investigators to conclude that awareness of congruence between lip movement and speech sound must be innate. It is all the more impressive (or baffling) if you assume that these babies, one to three months old, do not understand a word that is being said.

This talent for congruity jumps right over language barriers. For example, Scottish babies presented with Japanese faces and language sounds will eventually settle on the Japanese faces that are in synch with the Japanese sound track they are hearing.

When only a few days old, French babies prefer to look at faces speaking French, and Russian babies prefer to look at faces speaking Russian. How can they prefer the look of their native language when they have only seen it for a few days? Mentally they seem to leap beyond their physical experience.

**Quick Study.** We have seen that newborns quickly copy adult gestures like tongue-thrusting, wide mouth-opening, and lip-pursing. To do this they must see the mouth, tongue, brows, and hands accurately, but no practice is required. When brand-new babies imitate adult expressions of sadness, happiness, and surprise, it would seem to require more than mere looking and copying. Their ability to do this without hesitation suggests that newborns already "know" these human expressions and are prepared for instant dialog with us.

Note that the dialog of imitation is not one of words; it is one of *looking.*

Looking at you can be a source of joy or distress to your newborn. Remember how upset week-old babies became when their mothers wore masks and remained silent during one feeding (see chapter 4). In an experiment with older infants, mothers were told to become silent and "still-faced" for three minutes. Within fifteen seconds the babies knew something was wrong and reacted with inquisitive looks, vocalizing, or reaching out. Depending on their age, the babies used different techniques to gain attention. If unsuccessful, they withdrew altogether.

Worse effects were observed when mothers were told to look "depressed." The babies cried in protest, looked away, and days later were still acting wary of their mothers. Psychologists directing this research were so awed by the results, the experiment was stopped.

A "conversation" with your infant is remarkably similar to one you might have with anyone, except for the words. The Harvard films of mothers and babies "talking" reveal this. For brief spurts, infants seem passionately engaged in the exchange, showing interest by purposeful movements, attention, facial expression and excitement, and various lip and tongue movements. As soon as mothers saw and responded to this display, the babies reacted by changing a gesture or vocalization—as if to take their turn in keeping the conversation going. Edinburgh psychologist Colwyn Trevarthen concluded that communicating is innate.

Your baby is born ready for intimate dialog, words or no words. This represents an extraordinary turnabout in our understanding of babies. We have always focused attention on their weaknesses and limitations. In size and lack of muscular development they appeared obviously unprepared for life. It would be a long time, we assumed, before babies could do the simplest physical things. Of course they were not capable of more complex interactions.

The truth is, babies are born ready for *social* functions before they are ready for the world of physical objects. Relating emotionally and communicating intimately come before handling and manipulating objects, mastery of social skills before mastery of physical skills. This revolutionary discovery calls for a reversal of priorities: relating to babies mentally while they are catching up physically. The same infants who would rather listen than eat are more ready to communicate than to sit up.

**Invisible Talk.** Magical things happen when babies and mothers are together. How they influence each other is not always clear; the communication is invisible but potent.

As noted in chapter 3, newborns given the opportunity to room-in with their mothers in the hospital learn day/night cycles in three days' time while babies kept in the nursery show no progress at all. When mothers room-in with babies, they learn their own baby's cry so quickly that by the second night they awaken only to this cry.

Close connections pay off. If a mother picks up a crying infant within ninety seconds, the infant will usually quiet down within five seconds. If the baby is not picked up in ninety seconds, the disruption may go on for fifty seconds more.

We have noted (in chapter 2) the magic of touch communication and heartbeat communication (babies gained more weight). Deprivation in this area can be tragic. Even well-nourished babies who do not receive loving attention tend to fade and die. Material benefits are not enough. In radiant-heated cribs, newborns cannot maintain the same mean skin and core temperature of those who are placed on their mothers' chests skin-to-skin, even when the surrounding temperatures are the same.

Mothers, without knowing *how,* regulate not only the temperature of their newborns but also their hormone levels, enzyme production, respiration, and heart rate. Babies of mothers with low heart rates generally sleep for longer periods of time, fall asleep faster, and cry less than infants born to mothers with higher heart rates—apparently the result of private tutoring in the womb.

Pediatricians Marshall Klaus and John Kennell, the pioneers of bonding, tell us that communication is under way between parent and baby from the first cry and the first look. They note that the sound of a baby's cry will increase the flow of blood to the mother's breast in preparation for nursing. When placed near the breast, the baby will look for and find the nipple. The baby's sucking triggers release of oxytocin, a hormone that stimulates contraction of the uterus and expulsion of the placenta and helps prevent hemorrhage. The baby's sucking also stimulates production of prolactin, a hormone that facilitates milk production. In return, the mother's first milk (colostrum) is a transfusion of life-saving elements to protect the baby from many diseases. In this exchange, baby and mother take turns helping each other.

Breast-feeding holds promise of further communion as it brings you and your baby into range for perfect viewing. Your baby's potent gaze will help turn on a whole set of mothering skills, without which you might feel strangely inept and uninvolved with this new person in your life. This all-important bond is a friendship with mutual benefits, fostered by communication.

The art of communication takes a delightful turn at about two months of age. At this time your baby will display a talent for joint visual attention—that is, for looking at the same object you are looking at. First, the baby fixes intently on you while you are turning attention elsewhere. Then, seconds after you locate a new visual target, your baby turns to fix on the same target—two people focusing on a matter of common interest.

Infants calculate this so accurately, they skip right over identical targets put along their scan path by investigators trying to distract them. Undeterred, their eyes land on the object mother is looking at. This behavior, added to all the other examples of invisible gifts of communication, should help destroy yet another myth about babies—that they are egocentric. You will no doubt rejoice at every sign of social grace and sensitivity your baby shows. The need for the gifts of communication—friendly, intimate, instant, invisible, or verbal—is lifelong.

# PART TWO

## *Babies Remember Birth*

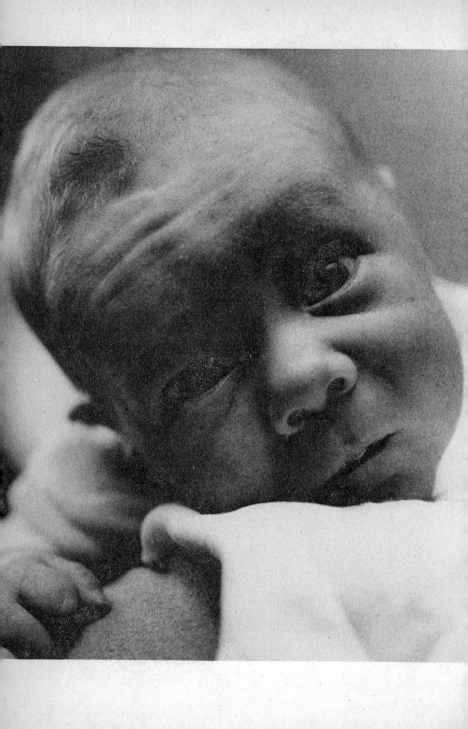

## CHAPTER 6

# Discovering Birth Memory

Although the idea of babies remembering birth seems a recent one, birth memories have shown up periodically for the last hundred years, accidentally and uninvited in doctors' offices. They have puzzled patients and doctors alike. Because they were not supposed to exist, they were something of an embarrassment. The memories often took a disguised form as recurring dreams, thoughts, habits, fears, or other phenomena that begged for understanding and resolution. Birth memories have come forth in response to hypnosis, psychoanalysis, LSD, psychodrama, submersion in water, and yogic breathing techniques. In unexpected ways they continue to make their way into conscious awareness.

Mentions of birth memory began appearing in the 1890s. What was at first a trickle from an underground stream in scattered locations has become a torrent breaking out virtually everywhere. If you have recalled some part of your own birth experience, you are in a select but rapidly growing group. In this chapter we will look at some of those who discovered this important, hidden stream of memory.

Remembering birth may be a special feature of life in the twentieth century. If the people of antiquity remembered their own birth, little evidence of it can be found. It would seem that birth memories, if they did exist, went unrecorded, were kept private, or were dismissed as incredible, as they still are today. But if you ask your child (or even if you don't) it is possible that he or she will share some memory of birth with you as soon as talking is possible.

In the late nineteenth century when physicians were learning the advantages of putting people into a sleeplike trance and making "suggestions" for medical improvement, a few made a surprising discovery. Some subjects in trance could regress in memory to earlier and earlier times, even to birth and life in the womb. Experiments in Paris and New York left tantalizing records but no verbatim accounts. The idea itself seemed so farfetched, it received little scientific attention. Hypnotic explorations of birth consciousness remained little more than a parlor game until the middle of the twentieth century.

However, the idea of birth memories was kept alive by a handful of therapists, most of them psychoanalysts, disciples of Freud. With strong convictions about the influence of early life experiences in the development of psychological problems, these therapists sometimes discovered dream images and behavior patterns in their clients that seemed related to birth. Freud popularized the idea of conscious and unconscious parts of the mind to explain everyday processes of remembering and forgetting. Freud wrote that we only "forget" things on a conscious level, while the real memories are stored in the unconscious, where they go on influencing us for years. We "act out" our buried memories, repeating the behavior over and over without realizing the real cause.

While he was busy treating clients suffering from various fears, compulsions, and anxieties, Freud speculated that traumatic birth could be the prototype for outbreaks of these feelings later in life. Freud thought adult anxiety could represent the trace of some previous upheaval, which might be a traumatic birth. He was not one to consider all births traumatic, but he acknowledged that there was always some risk of birth becoming so.

Freud stopped short of believing there could be a real self

or mental life active at birth, so when his patients had any type of birth memory he considered it a fantasy constructed by the mind at a later time. This view was adopted by psychoanalysts generally and has changed little in the years since.

Another visionary therapist who saw links between birth and many life problems, was Otto Rank, a friend and early associate of Freud. Rank went far beyond Freud (much too far, Freud thought) in believing that virtually all psychological problems, if not all human behavior, could be understood as reactions to trauma at birth.

Rank saw the womb as a primal paradise painfully lost in the separation at birth. Accordingly, he thought all later pleasure-seeking actions were attempts to reexperience the pleasure of the womb. In his view, the game of hide-and-seek recapitulates the seriousness of separation from mother and the pleasure of finding her again. All swinging games repeat the rhythm felt in the embryonic state—mothers walking about, starting and stopping, working and resting. Phobias of tunnels, travel, and being trapped repeat the anxiety of birth. Even sleep and sex were considered unconscious attempts to return to the darkness and pleasure of the womb.

These views of Rank were considered radical in 1924 and are regarded so by the majority of psychiatrists today. His premise that the womb is always a paradise is now questionable since modern studies provide evidence that suffering can take place in utero. However, Rank's brand of psychoanalysis, concentrating on birth, reduced the time required for therapy from several years to between four and eight months, a sign that he was onto something important.

At midcentury an innovative American analyst, Nandor Fodor, described many examples of adult memory flashes, dreams, or symptoms linked with birth. Birth events kept showing up in his patients' symptoms. A man, born on the

Fourth of July and subjected to a bedlam of loud sounds in the first twenty-four hours of his life, developed an abnormal fear of firecrackers. Another, born at home near railroad tracks, was hypersensitive to train whistles. One had painful reactions to bright lights apparently related to an operation on his skull at birth. An adult, born in a cold environment, complained of being chronically cold.

Fodor also ran into cases where uncanny feats of timing were apparently carried out unconsciously. Headaches, insomnia, and specific fears were associated with the day and hour of birth. One client had headaches at 2:00 P.M. on Fridays, the time of his birth. Another had a peculiar dread of 2:00 A.M. He could not bring himself to stay up until that hour and felt increasingly depressed at its approach. As a child he used to awake frightened and crying at 2:00 A.M. This turned out to be the exact hour of his delivery. Fodor speculated that such routine painful awakenings from sleep were flashbacks of pain associated with birth.

When Fodor's clients made the connection between their symptoms and birth trauma, therapy was successful. Along with Rank, Fodor viewed birth as an agonizing ordeal for the baby, a transition he compared to dying. He believed birth was so traumatic that we all develop a protective amnesia about it. The real memory is preserved in the unconscious mind, he believed, and emerges in dreams and behavior.

Fodor was puzzled when patients seemed to relive birth right there on his analytic couch. Like others, he could not quite accept that a real mind had been active at birth or that actual memory was responsible. He called birth stories "organismic impressions" and compared them to the rings in the cross-section of a tree marking the course of its physical growth.

To Fodor prenatal trauma was as common as birth trauma. He was concerned about possible shocks to the fetus during sexual intercourse late in pregnancy and by attempted abortions. He sensed that fetal consciousness could be affected by telepathic communication from the mother—communication from one mind to another.

By 1950, L. Ron Hubbard, the controversial founder of the Church of Scientology, developed a method of lay counseling (called auditing) that, among other things, frequently uncovered birth memories. His handbook of techniques for "auditors" taught a method of tracing symptoms back to their origins, some of which were at birth or in the womb.

In Hubbard's terms, he found that people were capable of going into a mental state called "dianetic reverie" (not hypnosis) in which they could have access to painful "recordings" (not memories) "locked" in the cells of the body.

Subsequently, millions of copies of his books have been sold, and uncounted thousands of people have remembered birth. The Scientology movement has popularized the idea that birth memory is real and may be associated with equally real problems.

Hubbard became convinced that birth had a critical impact on personality and that life in the womb had an even greater impact. Auditors found, for example, that asthma, eye inflammation, and sinus problems were often associated with experiences at birth.

During dianetic reverie, Hubbard claimed, people could relive traumatic incidents that had occurred at any stage of cellular development from zygote to newborn. With the help of an auditor, persons could be either "relieved" or completely "cleared" of their problems, although one hundred to five hundred hours of work might be required, depending on the number of traumas to be dealt with.

Although no formal program of research to verify birth memories was attempted, Hubbard was elated to report that the recordings of a mother and child pair in dianetic therapy compared "word for word, detail for detail, and name for name."

In 1970 psychologist Arthur Janov published the first of his books on primal therapy. Like Rank, Janov believed that early hurts in life (primal pain) were the foundation of most mental problems. In his therapy, Janov worked to evoke primal pain by intensive means until it was fully felt and slowly integrated by the patient. Birth pain was given special priority because it was considered the most devastating, required the most time to treat, and when completely treated showed the highest correlation with therapeutic success.

In primal therapy, recovery of feelings is the top priority, since these feelings are thought to be the key to behavior and illness. Birth memories as such are not sought or expected. A primal session, in which people act out and express feelings, is wordless because, as Janov believes, word recognition is not part of one's birth. For that reason, birth records from this type of therapy are reflective self-portraits of people looking back on birth experiences with insight. They make definite connections between their birth experiences and their physical and emotional problems. Janov provides abundant documentation of these connections in *Imprints: The Lifelong Effects of the Birth Experience.*

Birth memories, deeply hidden in the unconscious mind, usually announce themselves indirectly. They appear in association with some triggering event, such as watching people fall through space in a movie, seeing someone pinned down in a fight, or perhaps just watching a fish wriggling and struggling on a fishing line. The extreme feeling of anxiety stirred up by these events calls attention to the significance of the memory hiding at deeper levels of consciousness.

Dreams can expose hidden birth memories—for example, dreaming of being enclosed in a narrow underground tunnel, being underwater and fighting to get to the surface, or struggling mightily to reach the top of a hill but never making it.

Janov observed that repeated use of certain phrases and expressions could represent a breakthrough of birth memory, expressions like "My head is up against a wall," "I can't break through," "I'm in a tight squeeze," "I can't see daylight," "can't get started," "can't find my way out," "don't know which way to turn," "can't do anything right," or "just can't get enough." Frequent use of words like *pressed, pulled, gripped, weighed down,* or *pushed* may also carry overtones of birth.

A method introduced by psychologist Leslie LeCron, dating back to 1953, led to additional revelations about the connection between birth and later illness. The special usefulness of this method was its indirectness in bringing up information from an unconscious level of memory. In contrast to Janov's method, which gives priority to feelings, LeCron's method gives priority to information, quickly obtained, and with a minimum of emotional upset.

LeCron found that clients, usually in a light trance, would respond unconsciously to questions about their condition with signals from their fingers, representing "yes," "no," and "I don't want to answer." Called ideomotor signals because they seem to represent a mind-body signal, LeCron's finger signals are often used in hypnotherapy today.

Working closely with LeCron and using the finger signaling method, obstetrician David Cheek of San Francisco identified many birth and prenatal conditions that played a role in causing illness. In 1975 Cheek reported that in every instance of gastrointestinal pathology he explored, he found that the mother had been unwilling or unable to breast-feed. This included cases of peptic and gastric ulcer and spasms of the esophagus and colon. Respiratory problems such as asthma, emphysema, and hyperventilation were often associated with general anesthesia given the mother or with experiences of suffocation and panic at delivery. A case of migraine headaches was traced back to a forceps delivery.

In his extensive practice, Cheek also found that many female problems such as sterility and frigidity, painful or difficult menstruation, habitual abortion, premature labor, and toxemia were sometimes linked to a feeling of being unwanted or the "wrong" sex at birth. He reasoned that babies had apparently "imprinted" (a kind of instant learning) on such remarks as "We wanted a boy this time" or "We did not select a name for a girl." As grown-ups these women continued to distrust any demonstrations of appreciation and had trouble accepting compliments.

The LeCron method of communication with unconscious memory can sometimes trigger rapid progress in overcoming psychological difficulties. Using hypnosis and finger signals, Cheek was able to help a fellow passenger on an airplane who suffered from painful angina. Through answers from the unconscious provided by the fingers, Cheek discovered that the pain (which showed up only after the death of the man's mother) had been imprinted at birth when he heard his mother screaming. He had blamed himself for hurting her. This led to a pattern of guilt and concern over hurting people, and ultimately to self-punishment manifesting itself in heart pain. Once these revelations were placed in context, and the traveler learned how to bring on and take away the pain through hypnosis, the problem appeared resolved—all before the plane landed.

Birth also proved to be the source of trouble for a compulsive overachiever. This man, although unusually productive and successful, could never achieve a sense of self-worth. He had been born prematurely at seven and a half months and weighed only 3.5 pounds. Resolution of his problem of fifty years came when he remembered the doctor saying to the nurse, "Don't waste too much time. I don't think he is worth saving." This haunting remark had somehow become his inspiration for overachievement.

As a result of a very different type of therapy making experimental use of the drug LSD, psychiatrist Stanislav Grof found his clients constantly returning to aspects of their birth experience. Grof developed the conviction that labor and delivery exerted a profound and lasting effect on personality. During one session, a patient reported hearing distant human voices laughing and yelling and sounds of carnival trumpets. Later, his mother independently verified that this was a womb memory. She had attended the annual village fair, against the advice of her mother and grandmother. According to them, it was the noise and excitement of the fair that precipitated the delivery—a story the patient denied ever hearing and one his mother did not remember telling him.

Since his pioneering work with LSD, Grof has developed a system of "holotropic" therapy in which—by a variety of sounds, music, and movements—memories of childhood, birth, and before birth are evoked without drugs. Because this therapy is more centered on feelings, birth memories in narrative form are rare, though birth insights are common.

In 1977, an important lay movement, "rebirthing," began with the book *Rebirthing in the New Age* by Leonard Orr and Sondra Ray. In this system, breathing is the method used to evoke traumatic moments of the past, including birth. Breathing and repeated positive affirmations are then used to resolve these traumas. For example, an affirmation used by someone who was the "wrong" sex (as far as the parents were concerned) might be: "My sex is right for me," or "Thank God I am a man/woman."

Rebirthers share with Grof and Janov the idea that virtually all birth is traumatic, as well as the idea that birth is such a sensitive time that whatever happens then is likely to create a lifelong pattern. For example, a person born prematurely acts differently in the same situation than a person who was born late. Unwanted children may invite rejection, those breech-born may go at relationships backwards, the cesarean-born have trouble completing things, and incubator babies may grow up acting as if they are separated from love by a glass wall. In a book on birth and relationships, variations in birth conditions are related to disturbed patterns of relationship.

According to rebirthers, important patterns of thought are created at conception and during pregnancy as well as at birth. Scattered somewhere in this territory they expect to find evidence for the first negative views of self that afterward operate as "personal laws"—for example, "I can never get what I want when I want it." These serve to restrict behavior and have a pervasive influence. One of the main purposes of rebirthing is to neutralize this conditioning. For this, a series of dry or water sessions is usually necessary, followed by training seminars.

Rebirthing sessions do not ordinarily result in narrative birth reports. Impressions that arise during breathing crises are often hard to put into words. As is the case in other feeling-oriented therapies, a verbal description of birth is not the real concern.

Truly narrative moment-by-moment birth reports are rare, perhaps even unique; one looks in vain for them in published records. Using hypnotic memory techniques, cogent, detailed accounts of birth do emerge. These rather amazing stories have all the advantage of mature language (since the babies have grown up) but they reveal lucid thought processes and deep feelings which were going on in the infant at the time of birth. From them, we can learn what birth is like from the baby's point of view.

## CHAPTER 7

# *Little Children Remember*

**B**irth memories, if not entirely explainable, have a way of forcing themselves on us. They come in a variety of disguises such as those discovered by therapists treating nightmares, headaches, breathing problems, and phobias related to birth. Most disarming of all birth memories are those expressed by very young children. Inspired by some feeling, experience, or association, toddlers may surprise their parents with explicit memories of birth. Like the children themselves, these memories are innocent, unpredictable, and spontaneous, and they constitute an important new body of evidence for the reality of birth memory.

A small collection of such stories, gathered by Linda Mathison of Seattle, has opened this new window on the mind of the newborn. I am grateful to Linda and other colleagues for permission to share some of their stories with you. As more of us begin to question our children and listen to what they have to say, these reports will become more common. Readers are invited to send me copies of birth memories reported by very young children.

Usually appearing between the ages of two and three when children begin to talk, such reports can be startling and persuasive. Put yourself in this family vignette, for example. Your two-year-old son is lounging in the bathtub. All of a sudden he says there were many things he did not understand about his birth. Why were the lights so bright when he was new, he asks. Why was the light circular and intense where he was but dim elsewhere?

He poses one probing question after another. Why was the bottom half of people's faces covered by a green patch? Why did someone feel his anus with a finger, and why did they insert into his nose a tube that made a loud sucking noise? His questions turn to complaints. He didn't like the liquid put in his eyes that made it impossible for him to see, and he didn't like being put in a plastic box and taken somewhere.

This child does not know what green surgical masks, suctioning devices, surgery lights, or silver nitrate solution are. The only time he has seen these were at his own birth. Such an outburst of birth memory might mystify you, as it did the parents in this case, the father a college professor and the mother a child psychiatrist.

This bright child spoke about the "funny" opening of the wall of the uterus like a window (it was a cesarean delivery). He confided that there were many times he felt cramped and squeezed by the "walls" of the womb, though he perceived very dim light coming through them. His mother, an enthusiastic folk singer, had noticed during late pregnancy that the baby became more active when she sang loud low notes. At the time, she interpreted this as a sign of enjoyment. Part of her son's report in the bathtub, however, included a complaint that those loud low notes had been painful to him.

(An interesting update on this story: when the mother proposed to give a formal paper on these spontaneous birth memories at a psychiatric convention, her colleagues rejected the idea as frivolous.)

After children learn to talk, birth may be one of the first things they want to talk about. This impulse will not last long, perhaps only a year or two, before forgetting sets in. You have to go hunting for these memories while they are still within range.

You might like to conduct your own survey of children this age. Make sure the mood is relaxed and you have their attention. Just ask gently, "Do you remember your birth?" Bear in mind that a child's vocabulary is limited but the memory may still be fresh. Watch for demonstrations of knowledge in pointing, gesturing, drawing, or other nonverbal descriptions.

A San Diego man told me a story about his daughter. When she was two years old, he asked her if she remembered what it was like before she was born. She replied, "It was like this . . ." and assumed the exact position he remembered from an X ray taken just before her birth. The X ray, prompted by peculiar labor and fetal distress, revealed a "frank breech" position, a kind of jackknife position with the baby's bottom in the pelvis instead of her head. The doctors had showed it to the father to gain his permission for a surgical delivery.

Children have their own words for the sounds they hear before birth, like "broom-broom," "moo-din, moo-din," or "poon-poon." They speak of being born "in the water" or a "pond," of "swimming," and coming out through a "tunnel" to bright light and cold. In an obvious reference to the umbilical cord, one girl said, "There was a snake in there with me . . . It was trying to eat me but it wasn't poison, wasn't a poisonous snake." One described birth as being "in a light bulb; it broke."

Cesarean children come through a different doorway. One boy said he came out by himself when there was a big cut made by the doctors. He also described the circular motion "round, and round, and round" used to apply antiseptic before incision.

Children do not always describe things the way we do, but what they report may have unexpected validity. The same child who spoke of having a "snake in there with me" insisted there was a "doggie" in there also. She reported playing with the dog "like this" (waving her arms about) and hearing it bark. The improbable dog referred to was the family pet acquired as a puppy about five months before the baby was born. The mother said that the dog had spent much time in the latter part of her pregnancy right on her stomach.

Drawing pictures, acting out, and pointing to parts of the body are nonverbal ways that children may use to tell what they remember about birth. A child in Maine crayoned on a long roll of paper what looked like a fetus in the womb. Pointing to the drawing, he said, "Mommy, this is where I lived. This was me, Mommy, inside your tummy."

Another mother had this revealing conversation with her daughter at two years, seven months. They were sitting on a bed, the mother wearing some loosely tied sweatpants.

*Mother:* Do you remember when you were born, when you came out?

*Daughter:* Yeah.

*Mother:* Where were you before you came out?

*Daughter:* In there. *(Pulls open her mother's clothes and points to abdomen)*

*Mother:* Do you remember what it was like when you came out?

*Daughter:* Yeah . . . I was crying in Mama's butt. *(Again pulls open the pants and points to the perineum. This report was consistent with the fact that the baby cried as soon as her head came out, before the body was born)*

*Mother:* What else do you remember?

*Daughter:* *(Pauses; puts her hands on her mother's mouth, pulls the lips apart and back, spreads them)* Like that; it was like that.

*Mother:* Do you remember before you came out?

*Daughter:* Yeah. Little girl was swimming . . .

*Mother:* Do you remember if you saw anything when you came out?

*Daughter:* Genna and Donna [the midwives] and Daddy.

*Mother:* Do you remember anything else that happened?

*Daughter:* I was crying inside Mama's butt. In there. *(Pointing down inside her mother's pants)*

*Mother:* What happened after you came out?

*Daughter:* Genna fix my belly button.

*Mother:* Did you feel anything? How did you feel?

*Daughter:* I not feel. I guess I was okay. I was crying, though.

*Mother:* Did you hear anything when you were born?

*Daughter:* Genna said, "Donna, this baby's coming out." Yeah, Genna and Donna talking. Genna talking to me.

*Mother:* Do you remember anything else or anyone else?

*Daughter:* No, Mama. Dat's all.

Another child, two and a half years old, who had been bruised by forceps at delivery, was asked by her mother if it hurt to be born. She replied, "Yes! . . . like a headache." Another child, when asked if it hurt to be born, said "no" and pulled her arms and shoulders in close to her body in a squeezing motion.

Sometimes children volunteer information about birth without being asked. On a long car trip, a three-year-old Wisconsin boy suddenly asked from the back seat, "Mom, do you remember the day I was born?" Then he informed her that it was dark and he was up real high and couldn't get through "the door." "I was scared, so finally I jumped and got through the door. Then I was okay." The mother said the child's report was consistent with the fact that he had remained stuck high in the pelvis through some twenty hours of labor. Then things changed suddenly and he was born in a ten-minute second stage.

An anthropology professor, noticeably pregnant, was surprised by the following conversation with her daughter.

*Daughter:* Is the baby going to be dirty when she comes out of your tummy? I was dirty when I came out of your tummy in the hospital.

*Mother:* You were? What made you dirty?

*Daughter:* Mud. It was all over me. It was yucky!

*Mother:* What color was it?

*Daughter:* It was white.

*Mother:* What happened?

*Daughter:* They put me in the bathtub and washed me all clean.

*Mother:* And then what happened?

*Daughter:* They gave me to you and you held me. Then they took me and put me in a box. Why did they put me in a box?

*Mother:* To keep you warm. What did the box look like?

*Daughter:* It was a plastic box and it had a lid on it.

*Mother:* And what happened next?

*Daughter:* They brought me to you again and you held me.

*Mother:* Do you remember when we went home from the hospital?

*Daughter:* Oh yes. We went down some stairs and then we got in the car.

*Mother:* Where did you ride? In your car seat or in my lap?

*Daughter:* In your lap. I rode in your lap all the way home.

*Mother:* What happened when we got home?

*Daughter:* You put some pretty baby clothes on me and you put me in my crib and I went to sleep.

Another spontaneous revelation from the back seat of a car came from three-and-a-half-year-old Jason. On the way home one night, Jason said he remembered being born. He told his mother that he heard her crying and was doing everything he could to get out. It was "tight," he felt "wet," and felt something around his neck and throat. In addition, something hurt his head and he remembered his face had been "scratched up."

Jason's mother said she had "never talked to him about the birth, *never*," but the facts were correct. The umbilical cord was wrapped around his neck, he was monitored via an electrode in his scalp, and was pulled out by forceps. The photo taken by the hospital shows scratches on his face.

A two-and-a-half-year-old girl amazed her mother with an account of her birth. First she described her feelings, how cold she was, how many people were in the room, and what her mother and father were doing. Then she said, "Daddy was afraid to hold me, so he just looked at me and touched me. And you were crying, not 'cause you were hurt, but you were happy." The report was accurate, and the couple said they had never spoken to the child about the birth.

One girl, almost four, remembered a birth event that had been kept secret. Since no one in the family knew of it, they could not have told her about it.

Cathy had assisted the midwife in the home birth. After the delivery, when mother and baby seemed fine, the mother left the room to take a bath. The first midwife busied herself elsewhere. While Cathy was alone with the baby, the baby began to whimper. Instinctively, Cathy held her and offered her own breast. The baby suckled. When the mother returned, the baby was asleep. Cathy says she felt slightly guilty for being the first to nurse the child and said nothing to anyone about it.

Three years and nine months later, Cathy was baby-sitting a group including this child. In a quiet moment, Cathy asked the child if she remembered being born. She answered, "Yes!" and proceeded to give an accurate account of who was present and their roles during labor and delivery. She described the dim light of the womb and the pressures felt during birth. Then the child leaned up close and whispered in a confidential tone, "You held me and gave me titty when I cried and Mommy wasn't there." At that, she hopped up and went off to play. Says Cathy, "Nobody can tell me babies don't remember their birth!"

## CHAPTER 8

# Memories That Match

*Y*ou can't help wondering, as a parent, whether birth memories are real. Two questions are at issue: Are the memories what they seem to be (real and valid memories)? Are they reliable in the information they contain? Although absolute proof may not be possible at this stage of knowledge, research I conducted with ten mother and child pairs indicates that birth memories are real and reasonably reliable.

To determine the accuracy of what persons remembered about birth in hypnosis, I worked with pairs of mothers and their grown children. For research purposes, each had to be capable of hypermnesia (especially vivid and complete memory), and the children had to be old enough to speak easily about many details of birth. Mothers had to assure me they had never discussed details of the child's birth with the child, and the children had to have no conscious birth memories.

The children who qualified for this study ranged in age from nine to twenty-three; most were in their mid-teens. Mothers were from thirty-two to forty-six at the time of this work. Taking them in random order, I hypnotized them to whatever degree was necessary to achieve ease in memory.

To hold fantasy to a minimum, interrogation in hypnosis was conservative, avoiding leading questions and allowing subjects to speak freely. Reports were usually completed in a single session of one to four hours. Sessions of mother and child were held at different times, recorded on audiotape, transcribed, and compared.

The mother's memories of the birth experience, in hypnosis, were presumed to be generally reliable. By placing the child's birth memories beside the mother's I hoped to see how well they matched. If birth memories were only fantasies, as some contend, then the child's version would be likely to contradict the mother's report. If the child's birth memories were valid and accurate, they would echo each other at many points.

## Coherence and Consistency

Mother and child reports were coherent with each other, contained many facts that were consistent and connected, and were appropriately similar in setting, characters, and sequences. The independent narratives dovetailed at many points like one story told from two points of view. In some cases matching was uncanny.

Generally, reports validated each other in many details like time of day, locale, persons present, instruments used (suction, forceps, incubator), and type of delivery (feet or head first). Sequences of receiving bottled water, formula, or breast milk, appearance and disappearance of fathers, and moving in and out of different rooms were often consistent. Serious contradictions were rare. The table below indicates general characteristics of overlapping and serious contradictions found in the ten sets of reports.

Two daughters gave accurate descriptions of their mothers' hairstyles at the time. One mother described herself as "drunk" and disoriented by anesthetics during the birth; her

### Dovetailing and Contradictions in Ten Mother and Child Pairs

| Pair | 1 | 2 | 3 | 4 | 5 | 6 | 7 | 8 | 9 | 10 |
|---|---|---|---|---|---|---|---|---|---|---|
| Dovetails | 12 | 12 | 9 | 9 | 16 | 19 | 8 | 13 | 24 | 15 |
| Contradictions | 1 | 1 | 0 | 1 | 0 | 0 | 1 | 4 | 0 | 1 |

child said, "My mother was not all there . . . doesn't seem awake or have her eyes open." A boy whose mother reported that he was placed in a bassinet with plastic sides complained about "the shiny plastic or glass walls around me. Things look blurry, distorted."

**Onset of Labor (Pair #10).**  Facts recovered from the child: Mother was in the bedroom resting. It was daytime. Contractions started at 1:10 P.M. Mother telephoned father and the doctor and was advised to wait. Facts from the mother: At home in bed till 11:30 A.M. "About one o'clock I knew I was in labor and called my husband to come home. I telephoned the doctor; he advised waiting."

**At Reunion (Pair #10).**  Child reported, "Mother is talking and playing with me. There was a hassle [about the name]. My mom didn't like Virginia. She didn't like Ginger but daddy did." Mother reported, "I'm tickling and playing with her, stroking her . . . I want to name the baby Mary Kathryne and Bobby wants to name her Ginger."

**Delivery (Pair #1).**  Mother reported that "Michele was born very fast and they had to cut the cord off her neck. People were still putting drapes on my legs even while she was being born. And then she came the rest of the way out with another push." Child reported: "There is something bright, something big right over me. It's getting colder. I feel hands touching my neck, taking something off."

**Words and Names (Pair #1).**  Child reported hearing her name spoken and the words "I love you." Mother reported saying, "I love you" and hugging and kissing her and calling her Michele.

**At Reunion (Pair #6).**  Mother said, "I pick her up and smell her. I smell her head. I look at her toes and say, 'O God! She has deformed toes!' " She then asked the nurse about the toes and received assurance they were all right. The child said: "She's holding me up, looking at me . . . She's smelling me! And she asked the nurse why my toes were so funny . . . The nurse said that's just the way my toes were and that they weren't deformed."

## Error and Truth

There were various kinds of errors, small and large, in these narratives. For example, a mother said the birthplace was Bloomington, the child said Wilmington; a mother said the baby was wrapped with cotton, the child said paper. An aunt was mistaken for a grandmother, a father mistaken for a doctor (at the time this baby's father was an intern).

Some events matched but were out of order. Omissions —things remembered by one but not by the other—were intriguing. One mother confessed to making a nasty remark about the baby but the child did not report it. Is this omission an error, an act of mercy, or a memory so deeply buried it needs more uncovering?

**Contradictions.** Serious contradictions between the reports of mother and child were rare but did happen:

In Pair #1, the child associated breast-feeding with the delivery room, while the mother complained that this moment had been delayed by the hospital staff for a full twelve hours.

In Pair #10, the child reported breast-feeding while her father was in the hospital room. She even described his clothing, glasses, and hair and said, "Mother lets him hold me." However, the mother said fathers were not allowed in the rooms during feeding.

In Pair #7, the child said, "She holds me (in the delivery room) and starts kissing me . . ." According to the mother, the baby was laid on her stomach briefly, was taken to be cleaned up, was shown to her again, then placed in an incubator—all without touching.

In Pair #2, the son reported being held by his mother (after the delivery) and said she was smiling, very happy, and giggling. In contrast, the mother reported a feeling of helpless panic and fear of dying because the anesthesia had paralyzed her up to her neck. She said it was difficult to breathe or to tell anyone what was happening to her.

**Fantasy.**  The strongest evidence of fantasy in all the reports can be seen in four contradictions found in Pair #8. According to the child, her father's participation was traditional and normal, although her mother stated he was schizophrenic and not part of the scene. A favorite set of grandparents were also included in the child's narrative although in reality they were 3000 miles away. Aside from these glaring contradictions representing fantasies on the child's part, the mother and child agreed at thirteen points. This is important information. It means that fantasy can happen but may not affect the report as a whole. Fantasies were limited and specific.

**Complexities.**  Babies do not remember everything with equal certainty and force, and details are not always clear. For example, one child remembered leaving the delivery room: "I'm getting two things but they are different. The nurse carried me out. Then I'm in one of those little things they roll around. Maybe she carried me to the door." The mother's report simply said that they left the room together. All of the above could be true. We are dealing here with the inadequacy of verbal memory.

A baby may be awake and looking around one moment and asleep the next. Carried in a blanket, the baby's vision may be obstructed and then suddenly unobstructed. What the baby sees, therefore, may not be perfectly in synch with what the mother describes.

**Accuracy.**  Are these birth memories true? Taking the reports as a whole, they appear to be coherent, overlapping, and generally accurate. Flaws are apparent but seem more the exception than the rule, underscoring the natural limitations of human memory. Reports can be mainly valid yet contain some errors.

Some mistakes in memory are probably misperceptions to begin with (one baby thought he saw his doctor-father; it was really some other doctor). A memory mistake can also represent wishful thinking (wanting grandparents there), or creative fabrication to fill out a memory that is spotty. The unconscious mind might fabricate to hide or heal some painful aspect of the original situation (a mentally ill father).

Explaining accuracies is probably more important than explaining errors.

## Mother and Child Remember

In the following narratives, mother and child memories of the same birth are placed in sequence for comparison. They illustrate the coherence and dovetailing found in this research.

The narratives are from independent reports, in hypnosis, from two mother and child pairs. Matching details and sequences are a sign that the memories are not fantasies (which would be expected to diverge and contradict each other) but two stories of the same birth from different points of view.

At birth, mothers and babies have certain experiences in common, especially, during delivery, reunions in the hospital, and the journey home. The accounts of these events often dovetailed. The two also have well-defined individual interests, however. For example, a mother may dwell on external details related to getting a spinal shot, while the child tells about the inner world of contractions. A child may describe how the doctor wriggled and wrenched her neck pulling her out, while her mother may not have seen this or thought nothing of it.

The most obvious discontinuity in reports involves the period in the nursery. The child's memory of the sojourn here is usually a telling one, but it has no parallel in the report of the mother who was not there. Because of this, nursery narratives are omitted in this section.

### Linda and Her Mother

#### Beginnings of Labor

*Linda:* I feel my mother tense up and I tense up. Then I relax. I feel like I want to keep going but I just stay in place. I'm all squished up in there. When I'm all squished up I want to go forward, and when I relax I want to push myself back.

*Mother:* My husband wouldn't believe me that I was in labor. He didn't want to call the doctor, so I called the doctor and he told me to go to the hospital. I was glad it was time. My husband took me in the car.

*Linda:* She's walking . . . sitting down in a car or something. I'm in a funny position. I can feel the car vibrate.
It feels really uncomfortable because I'm already in a very uncomfortable position . . . I'm all cramped up. My shoulders are squished but my neck is twisted. I wanted to straighten it out but I can't.

#### In the Delivery Room

*Linda:* I guess she's on the table thing now. My mom's mad at someone, not me. She feels angry. I think it's a woman, not the doctor.

*Mother:* A woman is screaming, somebody in another room. She keeps screaming and it makes *me* want to scream! My nerves are jumpy. I'm trying to breathe, trying to go with my own feelings. I wanted to scream out and tell her to shut up! Her scream was not really from pain but just wanting constant attention.

*Linda:* She's lying on the table. It seems like everyone is anticipating, everyone is watching. I can't see them but I can tell they are there. My mom is wishing I would hurry up. I felt like she is thinking it is taking too long. I feel real tight but my neck isn't squished. Before, when she relaxed I sort of went back in. Now when she relaxes I stay in the same place and I don't go backward. My head is real tight but it feels not as tight on the top of my head.

*Mother:* The doctor comes in. I'm glad. He's very calm towards me. He asks the nurse some questions. It has to do with why it was so late before they called him.

They are getting ready for the spinal. I'm very uncomfortable on my back. It's hard to breathe. The contractions hurt. They bend my body while I'm on my side and the doctor gives me a shot.

## Delivery

*Linda:* I have twisted my head around, I don't know how. My head is a little bit out. I'm starting to turn my head to make it match my body because it was stuck over. I was worried about having my head straight.

The doctor is putting his hands on my temples. I want him to let go. I'm trying to push myself back inside because I don't like it. I feel frustrated, like I want to do it by myself. I want it to be *me* who does it. I don't want him to touch me. I feel pressure there. It might take a little bit longer but I'd feel more comfortable.

He didn't feel very gentle. He was just trying to get it over with. Then he pulled! It hurt my neck! Then he wriggled me around—something I don't trust! He pulled me away, held me up in the air out away from him. Then he hit me—not real hard—and I start crying.

I can tell my mom's wanting to have me by her, and I want to be there but there's nothing I or she can do about it. I want to fly over there but I can't. It's hopeless.

There's a machine or something . . . and they are putting it over my mouth. It was really weird, like a white tube machine. I think it was supposed to take stuff out of my lungs or something.

*Mother:* I can't feel the contractions anymore, just the pressure, not the pain. The doctor adjusts the mirror so I can see. I can see the black hair of the baby.

They're all talking about my next contraction. They want me to push. I don't feel it, so I don't know when to push. And the nurse gets up by me and pushes on my tummy. I think if I can just get through this it will be over soon.

The baby's head is through. There's a lot of black hair . . . All I think about is the baby now. He put his finger in her mouth to scoop stuff out. After this the nurse handed him a white syringe which he put in her mouth to draw out fluids.

The baby's born, and he tells me it's a girl. That's fine. I'm happy!

## On Mother's Stomach

*Linda:* They put me on my mother's stomach. I felt a lot better. I was trying to grab for her and she was looking at me.

I looked up at her. I wanted her not to let them take me away, but when I saw her face I knew she wasn't going to do that. Then I just give up.

Someone dries me off, wraps me in a blanket, and hands me over to the nurse, and she took me out into a little room. She laid me down in one of those little baby basket things. I guess they were taking a picture. I want to turn over and go to sleep . . .

*Mother:* Then they bring the baby and put her on my tummy. She's crying. They lay her across my tummy face-down. I think she's a beautiful baby. I cried. I love it that they've put her on my tummy. She's across my tummy with her head on my left side. I can look at the side of her face. She holds her head up to cry. I think I'm not supposed to touch her.

They take her away. I didn't like it but I figured that's the way it has to be. She quit crying. She is looking around.

They have her in a blanket. They put her in something with glass or plastic sides; it's over on the other side of the room.

## To the Nursery

*Linda:* I think I left first. My eyes are closed and I'm all curled up because they took me away from my mother. I'm wrapped in a blanket.

. . . [I went] to the room where all the babies go. I wanted to be with my mother. I could tell there were lots of other babies . . . and my mother wasn't there.

*Mother:* They are rolling me out with the baby, both of us beside each other. My husband is in the hall and he sees the baby. He just smiles. Tears are coming down my cheeks, and they take me to my room. They take the baby to the nursery. I wonder when I'll see her again. I want to hold her and look at her. I'm planning to nurse her.

## Reunion

*Linda:* The nurse was carrying me and passed one bed. I think mother was farthest from the door. Then I saw her. I felt good. I knew she was bringing me to her.

*Mother:* I occupied the bed farthest from the door . . .

*Linda:* Mom reached her hands out and took me. She hugged me and started nursing me. Feels nice. The nurse was standing there for a minute . . . She asked my mother something, like if she wanted something . . . and another person was in the room, another patient. I was paying more attention to being with my mother.

*Mother:* I turn on my side. I prop myself up on my elbow because they are going to lay her right beside me. I'm on my left side. They lay her down and I open up my nightie to feed her. The nurse is going to try to help me because she says some women have a hard time. I wish she'd just leave me alone. I tried to put her out of my mind and give my attention to the baby. There was no problem. She took the nipple right away. And the nurse left. She said how well I did.

*Linda:* I keep wanting to hug her but I can't. I just move my hands, hold onto things like her arm. She's telling me I'm a pretty baby. She's putting her fingers through my hair. She told me I had pretty hair. It made me feel good.

Part of the time she just looked and smiled. I felt she was glad, even though I caused her problems in the beginning. She didn't mind anymore.

*Mother:* And then I started to unwrap the baby and look at her legs and feet and talk to her. I said, "You're so pretty, Linda! Hi Linda! I love you. I'm your mommy."

## Going Home

*Linda:* They put me in a cloth bag [pouch]. My father is there. He seems unsure around me. It felt different being outside. Bright out there. I keep getting handed back and forth. My mother and father were helping each other. My father was going to drive home . . . They tell me I am going to see my house, and I know the nurse is not going to take me away [anymore].

*Mother:* I'm getting into the car to go home and the nurse hands me the baby. Ted is driving us home. I feel good. I know I can be a good mother. I'm glad to be in charge, on my own with the baby. I'm looking forward to showing her to my parents.

*Linda:* I'm looking around the inside of the apartment, going up some stairs . . . They put me in the bedroom. It wasn't just mine . . . It seems like there are people around. It felt a lot nicer being there than in the hospital.

*Mother:* We rented the upstairs of a big house in Whittier. My mother and father are there. Ted carried the baby upstairs [inside the house] . . . My father tells me what a fine baby she is. He looks very proud.

I put the baby in the crib. It was next to my bed. I had it all lined with a "bumper." She looked so small in there . . .

### Katy and Her Mother

#### In the Delivery Room

*Katy:* It's a pretty big room, with a lot of silver in it. Everybody seems pretty busy. I think there are four or five people. It seems colder than it did before. I feel like I'm spinning, turning too fast. They're pulling, pulling at me. The doctor is shaky . . . nervous . . . trembling, and it kind of bothers me.

*Mother:* It's a fairly large room, and chilly. I can see her head coming out of my vagina. There are two doctors. There's a young doctor [in green] and an older doctor with gray hair [in white]. There are nurses on the sides. The younger doctor is busy. They're checking the head . . . The head is out [now].

*Katy:* They put me on her stomach, sort of dumped me on her. He's talking to my mom. Everything seems to be okay and she's all right. He still seems nervous, and he picked me up and gave me to somebody else. I feel bigger and heavier. I can see her but I'm not by her. Her hair is wrapped up, like in curlers or something. She looks tired, sweaty.

*Mother:* They sort of put her on my stomach, but they're still holding onto her. I could see her . . . lots of blood and white stuff. She's crying. I can see the umbilical cord. My hands are fastened down because I can't reach out and touch her. I would like them to move her, wrap her up. Somebody does finally take her. I'm talking to the doctor . . . I think they had a white cap over my hair.

*Katy:* Nobody's talking to me. They're talking about me, I think, but not *to* me. They act like they know I'm there, but like *I* don't know I'm there. The nurse kind of wiped . . . washed me. Then they brought me over next to my mother. She wasn't crying, but something like that. She's the first one that talked to me. She said, "Hi!" Nobody else seemed to think that I was really there. Then she talked to the doctor a little bit and they took me away again.

*Mother:* They finally undo my hands and the nurse brings her over on my left side. But she doesn't hold her close enough so I can touch her. I really feel frustrated. I do say "Hi!" to her. She's so cute and small but still kind of messy. Then they put her in a little warmer. I talk to the doctor about her weight.

## To the Nursery

*Katy:* I didn't know where they were going to take me or why. I left the room before my mother did. I didn't see my dad much. He was around . . . but not much. I really didn't know exactly who he was until later.

Then they took me away again to a different room with lots of other people [babies]. It seemed kind of far. I was in there with a bunch of other babies and people kept coming in and bothering us, woke us up.

*Mother:* We were ready to leave. I'm on a gurney. They wheel her out first. We're down the hall. Her father's there, looks at her [but doesn't touch]. I don't remember going to bed but I'm in bed. I don't know what happened to the baby or to my husband. They put the baby in another room.

## Reunion

*Katy:* Sometimes they took me back to my mom but they always brought me back to the room [nursery] again. It was really neat. [Mom] seemed happy, comfortable. Her hair was down. I was tired, sleepy. I enjoyed nursing. A nurse was in and out. Everyone knew what was going on except me. I didn't know why they were taking me away or where I really was.

*Mother:* I'm in a two-bed room and the baby's all cleaned up. She's in a little plastic bed. They've moved her in, like rooming-in. I pick her up, unwrap her, get comfortable on the bed. She's looking me over. I'm talking to her . . . I nurse her. Then I put her back in her bed. Her father comes to visit [but doesn't touch]. At night they take her to the nursery.

## Leaving the Hospital

*Katy:* My dad came to get my mom with my sister and somebody else, another man, but I don't know who he is. My mom was in a wheelchair holding me. I have a blanket around me, silky, and it's got little pink flowers.

It seemed like a real long way. Everyone seems to be happy.

*Mother:* I'm getting organized. I am anxious to leave and I'm dressed. The baby is wearing soft flannel pants with feet and a little top. It has little rosebuds down the front. Her father comes and tells me that our daughter and my brother-in-law are waiting downstairs. The nurse comes. I sit in a wheelchair, holding the baby.

It seems like a long ride. It's taking a long time to get home. There's a lot of joking and light conversation.

*Katy:* I was in a white crib . . . and there was something hanging over my head. I thought it was pretty weird at first but I got used to it.

*Mother:* I put the baby in her bassinet. She's not asleep but seems really happy there. I think we had a mobile attached to it.

Three theories are regularly advanced to explain birth memories. Some suspect that child memories are mother-memories in disguise, passed on to the child at unguarded and forgotten moments through childhood. This theory is plausible but not consistent with what the memories contain: things not seen or known by the mother in the first place, or things she would not want to tell. Occasionally a child's memory, rather than the mother's, is verified as the correct one. Also, the words used are usually not the technical words preferred by adults.

A second common theory is that birth memories are fantasy quilts made up of bits and pieces of information gathered and sewn together long after birth. Such fantasy productions would surely be more stereotyped and predictable than the birth stories I have heard. In my ten pairs, fantasy was easily spotted and was rare. It cannot explain the realities common to both reports.

Finally, some believe that babies do not understand what is said at birth until they learn language, and thus see birth trauma as retroactive. This theory of delayed effect disregards the evidence for meaningful communication at birth.

In every other respect life seems to be progressive, not retroactive. Babies spanked now do not react later. Evidence for skillful communication at birth does not suggest an intellectual delay.

Considering all the facts, objectively gathered birth memories appear to be genuine recollections of experience. The birth memories of my ten pairs certainly seem to be real memories, not fantasies; personal memories, not mother-memories; and are more often true than false. Within reasonable limits, these memories were a reliable guide to what happened at birth.

CHAPTER 9

# *Birth: As Babies See It*

*B*abies, interviewed as adults under hypnosis, have much to tell us about birth in our time. In content their memories vary, as all personal stories do, yet they eloquently express many common feelings and concerns. These witnesses tell the inside story of things hidden from view before delivery. They also tell the outside story of events in the delivery room and hospital nursery that can be verified by parents, nurses, and doctors.

Reports of how babies feel in the first minutes and hours outside the womb are consistent with the feverish communication so common at hospital birth: loud cries, pained facial expressions, flailing of arms and legs, the body shuddering and shivering. Happily, at times their verbal reports tell of something infinitely better: gentle handling, a warm, tearful embrace, radiant grins, and unbroken bonds.

For most babies these days, onset of labor is followed by an uncomfortable trip to a hospital, head squeezed against the car seat. Activity at the hospital is remembered as a series of the mother's moves in and out of wheelchairs, beds, and rooms, and encounters with nurses and doctors. Babies show concern when fathers are missing, observe whether mother feels nervous or calm, and evaluate the attitude and behavior of birth attendants.

## Labor, from Inside

The first contractions of the uterus, which signal onset of labor to the mother, signal also a change in lifestyle for the passenger inside. At first, babies experience the muscle contractions as "ripples of pressure," "pulsations," or "like being in a ship on a rocky sea." As they progress, the contractions are recognized as serious and lead to new movements, pressures, positions, and turns. This overpowering force is described as a "rush of energy," "a river," or "tidal wave." If labor is too fast it is "like going down a slide backward; you go *sloop!*" said Diana. Baby Annette came so fast she slipped through the doctor's hands—something we discovered while investigating her fear of flying.

### Glenda

Going to the hospital in the car. On the seat inside my mother. My head is being squeezed.

Father's not there. I feel unsafe and uncomfortable. My mother's mad. She wished I wasn't there. This all seems crazy! It should be a happy time.

### Theresa

It's dark . . . I'm getting a rush of energy. I'm feeling really tense; a lot of energy! Every muscle is tense, but I'm not going anywhere. I'm just staying there . . .

I'm anxious. It's getting light and I'm getting a headache. I feel like I'm going to explode! I feel like everything is rushing to my head.

I feel more down than up; I don't know how to describe it. I feel I am on a slant board with all the blood rushing to my head . . .

Marianne admits she was resisting birth. She wasn't ready and wouldn't go along, she said. Nevertheless, she found herself attached to an irresistible "tidal wave."

## Marianne

They said it's time to be born. I feel the pressure but I don't want to be born. I'm not ready yet. I'm just going to wait; it feels much better in here.

Now they are coming faster, faster; this way, that way. Oh, it's getting intense! It's pushing, pushing, pushing me out. I want to stay right here where I am, but they insist.

It feels like a tidal wave . . . I can see that I'm attached to the tidal wave. When it's ready to go, I guess I have to go, too . . . Oh-oh, the tidal wave is coming again.

I'm still not ready. It's pushing, pushing. I'm going to stay right here. I don't want to go anyplace, but I have to . . ,

Oh-oh, they are putting on gloves. They are getting me. Oh, goodness sakes, grrrr, that was a squeeze!

They are holding my head, but gently; they were gentle. And next thing I know, they're saying, "You just lie right here," and they wrap me up in something.

## Life in the Delivery Room

When labor is over and babies are outside breathing on their own, they experience new sensations, emotions, people, and places. Coming from an environment of extreme closeness, literally "touched on all sides," they sometimes complain of feeling "lost in space!" One boy found the birth room "hectic and confusing."

Virtually all babies complain about bright lights, cold rooms and instruments, the noise, rough contact with their sensitive skin, and nearly every medical routine including slaps, injections, eye drops, hard scales, being held in midair and handled by strangers. Babies dislike forceps, sometimes fear incubators, and think the masks worn by nurses and doctors make them look "alien." They strenuously object to the way the umbilical cord is cut, not that it hurts necessarily, but they report anxiety about *how* and *when* this vital connection is severed.

Babies express gratitude for gentle handling and kind words from nurses and doctors. Above all, they are grateful for immediate contact with their mothers after delivery.

### Mary

The doctor has me, and I'm looking at my mother. I'm glad to see her and she's glad to see me . . . She looks pretty. She's all sweaty and frazzled but she looks young, good. She feels good; she's smiling. It's a happy time.

I hear somebody saying, "That's my girl." I feel my mother is always telling me I'm a good girl. She's happy with me, pleased with me.

The doctor is talking, giving orders to people, telling them to cut this, get that . . . He has a nice voice; he's a nice doctor, an older man. He's pretty gentle.

### Scott

I'm kind of scared of all the people. It's new; I'm not used to that . . . I would like to get out of this delivery room. I don't like to be here because of all the people, lights.

The environment isn't safe, isn't secure for me . . . There's so much openness! I'd rather be in a smaller, cozy room.

### Marcie

I feel I'm being pulled out, head first, gasping for air. Somebody is cutting the cord. It's a strange feeling to be out in the air where all of a sudden I'm kicking and moving my arms. It's like being in a big open space; it's frightening.

I don't like the looks of the people with masks covering their faces. I keep staring at their masks. My mom is the only normal looking one in the room!

Everything is foreign. I feel out of place, like I don't know what to do. Space is overwhelming!

I want to be back with mother.

When they pulled me out I felt turned upside down. Someone smacked me on the butt. I started screaming and they turned me right side up again. I didn't like being upside down at all!

Then they put me on a table—really weird, very foreign. I felt like I shouldn't have been there. There is someone wiping me off.

Everything everybody is doing to me had never been done before; it was all new and it all felt funny. They put me on a table on my back; felt weird.

Struggling . . .

The most universal complaint of newborns is about being separated from their mothers.

## *Anita*

There are lights, bright lights. And a man with a mask and funny hat on. He has gloves on and they feel funny.

The lights are too bright for my eyes. I'm moving my arms. And now my legs are out and I'm crying.

They handed me to someone, a lady. It's cold.

The surroundings are so new it's frightening. I can't hear my mother. I can't feel my mother; that's frightening.

Then I felt my mother. Not like before, but it was her —for just an instant. And they took me away.

I was taken to a room and put down. The lights were very, very bright. They were cleaning me, wiping me . . . Then they put me on something like a bed.

Before that they put me on a scale; it was real cold. I

was crying but they didn't pay attention. They were
doing their work . . .

I was in bewilderment about what was happening! I
thought they were mean. I wanted my mother. I can't see
her.

They have left me alone . . .

### Theresa

Someone is wheeling her [mother] away. I don't understand why they are doing it. I feel like I am all by myself
with them in a big room.

She's gone. They took her. I'm mad! It seems so stupid.
There isn't any reason why she couldn't stay . . .

The following witnesses, Lynn and Emily, complained
about needles and eye drops.

### Lynn

A nurse in a white cap comes, picks me up, and bounces
me all around. She takes me over to a table and unwraps
the blanket. Oh, that feels good!

Then she washes me down. That's kind of cold.

The needle hurt. She puts alcohol on me and puts a
needle in my bottom.

She's smiling and talking, very quick and efficient. She
changes me and wraps me back up in the blanket. I don't
like this. It was nice to be held.

She picks me up and bounces me again . . .

### Emily

It's so cold in my eyes, and my head still hurts. They're
laughing because I'm crying.

And my mother's voice is excited. She's saying she wanted a girl.

She's wanting to see me . . . She sees the birthmark on my leg and she says, "She's mine all right; she's got my mark on her leg!"

## Strong Feelings about Nurseries

With rare exceptions, babies feel distressed and lonely when placed in a nursery. One child said, "There was nobody around I belonged to. I felt abandoned." Others are disoriented, baffled, bored, even outraged. Grief is the prevailing emotion. It is catching, and the other babies often wail in concert!

Babies complain of being wrapped tightly when they want to move, being on their backs when they want to be on their stomachs, and having to wait to be fed when they are already hungry. They develop headaches, earaches, cold feet, become jealous, angry, or depressed. Some escape cruel realities by daydreaming. Sandra, weary from nine months "on a stormy sea," wishes she could make the nurses understand all she had been through but, sadly, she cannot get their attention.

For Helen, a small town nursery was a heavenly place to be, thanks to a happy nurse—a singing, humming, loving nun. Winter snow had prevented her mother from going home to their isolated ranch, so Helen had the pleasure of several weeks in this special environment.

### *Helen Has a Singing Nun*

There's a room with a nun in it. She has a blue and white dress, and a big hat with wings that come out on the side.

It's a nursery. She's singing, just humming to herself. She loves the babies. There are only two other babies there and many empty bassinets.

It's comfortable there. It's been awhile; it seems like I belong there. She's very nice to us.

She likes me. I'm a healthy, strong baby. I'm bigger than the others and easy to care for.

I keep seeing the nun. She's so happy all the time! I can tell that she really loves us. She does everything: keeps us clean, feeds us.

It's nice being held by her, soft and warm. Feeding us isn't a chore; it's a pleasure for her. She talks to us and hums. Never hurries. It's like we belong to her.

It's a very peaceful time.

### Sandra

I'm in the nursery.

The nurses are around the other babies. I feel disappointed that they don't know what I've been through. They are just ignoring me.

I've been through something very unpleasant for a long time. They don't understand it. I think it would help if they knew.

They were friendly but they didn't spend much time with me. They kept fussing around this one baby—five or six nurses. They just aren't paying any attention to me.

I feel cold. I wondered what was wrong with me, what to do to get them to pay attention. But I figure they don't want to pay attention to me; they don't consider me important.

I keep seeing the nurses around that one bed. That baby must be really something! They are all around, with their heads bent over, watching that baby.

They are so interested in watching that baby!

I keep feeling left out. *(Sigh)*

For Dee and Brenda, being in the nursery means loneliness, boredom, and depression.

## *Dee*

I'm being put down in a little bed. I feel like I'm left alone
. . . I feel bad because no one is holding me and I'm all by
myself.

Everything seems so big. I feel so small.

I'm all by myself . . .

## *Brenda*

I can't see anything. And I can't hear anything either. I
just lie there awake. I lie there for a long, long time waiting for something.

Waiting . . . and nothing is happening. It's very boring
. . . It's all quiet, and so alone.

It wasn't nice to be alone.

For babies who have had a difficult birth and are left with
serious concern about their health, the nursery is an even
more anxious place. Deprived of the constant and individual
care they would get from their mothers, they feel unsafe.
Group care means they are left in the hands of strangers who
are in and out of the room, have many babies to care for, give
only routine attention, and may not respond to their urgent
cries for help. They need the assurance that only a mother
can give.

Jeffrey, who had a problem breathing, describes his pre-
dicament in the nursery. He explains exactly how his mind
and emotions affect his physical condition. He speaks with
authority.

## *Jeffrey*

I feel secure and contented and safe when I'm held. I feel
vulnerable and fearful by myself.

I had a lot of trouble breathing, sometimes pain; mostly

a labored breathing. I had to work at it to breathe . . .
Sometimes it became very difficult to breathe.

The fear at these times is overwhelming!

I knew something was wrong . . . There were a couple
of times when the breathing became very difficult and
there was no one there to hold me.

When it's hard to breathe, being held helps a lot. It
helps the fear, then the breathing . . . Breathing becomes
very hard when there is no one there—which seems to me
a long period of time—and the longer it lasts the more
afraid I am.

Jackie and Sandy suffer emotionally, afraid they will not
be cared for. The care they feel they need is not what the
nursery staff provides.

### Jackie

They took me to a big room and put me in a little box,
gave me some brown stuff, vitamins or something, and
put stuff in my eyes. They looked into my ears and left
me there.

I was scared. I was all by myself.

### Sandy

I'm in a little bed. I'm cold and the back of my head hurts.
I'm lonely, nervous, shaky. I feel like I've been deserted.

They left me in the nursery alone.

As fathers well know, part of hospital birth is the familiar
glass window of the nursery that protects newborns from
the outside world (including fathers). Annette and Mary had
opposite feelings about seeing their fathers through the window. Mary and her father had a happy exchange, but An-

nette was left with a distinct impression that she was the "wrong" sex.

## Mary

[My father is] really silly. He's grinning. He's really silly.

He's grinning and he's excited. He's outside in another room, looking through the glass.

It's the first time I've seen him. He looks like a monkey! He's excited.

Then he gets to hold me. He's happy. *(Giggling)* I'm happy, too.

## Annette

I'm at the hospital, in the nursery. And I'm in the nurse's arms. She is holding me, showing my father that he has a little girl.

Well, I was supposed to be a little boy!

My dad was very disappointed. I was supposed to be Gordon. They had the name all picked out. And then they had to quickly decide a name for a girl.

He *knew* he was going to have a boy; he was positive of it.

## Reunion with Mother

Getting back in touch with mother after isolation in the nursery is a relief to most babies. They know they should be there with her but sense that in a short time they will be taken away again just as they were after birth. They brace themselves for a repetition of the earlier experience. The happy or unhappy quality of the reunion depends on the attitude of both mother and child.

### Susan Carries Resentment

They took me to see my mother. She was really excited.
She picked me up and was holding me. It felt good but I
was mad at her. She was really happy, but I didn't care
anymore. She deserted me. I was angry with her.

When she was holding me, when she was warm to me,
I forgot how mad I was.

### Jackie

In her room she is holding me, feeding me. I like that. I
feel safe. She talks to me. She tells me my name. She tells
me that she likes me and that I'm pretty. Then they take
me away again!

Dana's mother was twenty-one, unprepared for childbirth, and clearly nervous. She was doing her best, however,
and her love came through.

### Dana Understood Her Mom

She's holding me and I'm in a white blanket. She's looking
at me, touching me. I felt safe in her arms, warm. I felt
better . . . not closed in a box. I felt safer.

She was nervous how to hold me. She didn't know if
she was holding me right. She seemed uneasy but excited
and happy. She kept changing sides to hold me . . .

I see her in the hospital bed with propped-up pillows.
And she's sitting there feeding me (a bottle). It doesn't
taste that good. It tastes like vitamins . . .

I'm sleeping, very quiet. Comfortable.

## Nancy

The first milk was from the breast. And that was the worst! It tasted like anger. It had a bilious taste . . .

It's just that nobody liked me. Nobody wanted me.

Emily's reunion with mother after birth included a visit by father. As she listened to her parents talk, she felt like an object rather than a person and wasn't sure she liked them very much.

## Emily

I guess I'm in the same room [with her]. I can hear her voice and then my father's voice. They're excited talking about birth.

Then he comes and looks at me. But he doesn't pick me up. He just pokes me with his finger. He says something stupid like "Gootchie, gootchie."

He doesn't know I'm a person; I'm a *thing* called baby. He's saying, "That's all the babies; this one was hard enough."

I didn't think I was that hard.

I don't think I like these people very well. They give me a headache . . . They don't think I'm a person. I know I am.

## CHAPTER 10

# *Pitfalls*

*U*nder the pressures of childbirth and family relationships, feelings spill out and people may say things they later wish they could take back. Husbands blame wives, wives blame husbands, both may blame the baby, and sensitive babies sometimes blame themselves. This blame is illusory and irrational, but it hurts anyway. It is only one of the emotional pitfalls of birth.

Like the challenges of starting school, leaving home at eighteen, or retiring at sixty-five, birth has its hazards too. Nasty experiences during this delicate passage can leave harmful imprints, "birthmarks" that are psychological rather than physical.

As long as babies were thought to have no emotions, no developed senses, and no thoughts, concern about "birth trauma" seemed unjustified and attracted little attention. Now that babies are known to be intelligent, sentient beings, their mental and emotional vulnerability must be reconsidered.

Not every birth is a happy one. Through insensitivity to the newborn as a person, doctors, nurses, and parents can spoil the occasion with thoughtless ridicule, criticism, or morbid predictions about an infant's appearance or future. Therapists can tell you how often such gratuitous remarks turn out to be pathogenic—literally generating illness. Just as pregnant women should avoid contact with the chemical teratogens that create malformed bodies, those present at birth should avoid the psychological teratogens that foul infant minds.

Parents may leave emotional scars on their offspring by threats, rejection, or callous remarks betraying unresolved personal problems and issues. Pregnancy is an ideal time for healing body, mind, and spirit, so that problems are resolved well before delivery. Problems left unresolved can cause the baby immediate suffering and can upset family relationships for years to come.

For some newborns, the first encounter with mother, father, siblings, and other relatives is perilous. The environment in which they find themselves spawns fear, anger, depression, or shame. Even inside the womb, babies can sense the rumble of family warfare. Outside, they must learn to cope with unhappy parents, antagonistic relatives, jealous siblings, and frustrated medical personnel.

What mothers feel deeply and what they say and do to babies is extremely important. If they lack emotional support, mothers may find themselves with little to give their babies: little love, little milk, and little desire to mother. In unguarded, supposedly private moments, a parent may give vent to terrible feelings, untempered by reflection or restraint, while babies listen intently.

## The Impact of Rejection

The following stories will alert you to the harm that can be caused by various forms of rejection at birth. Shirley is rejected because she isn't the "right" sex—a complaint a number of patients have shared with me. The rejection faced by Glenda and David is one step worse, not being wanted at all. As a result, each feels deprived and sad. Had their mothers realized how astute the newborns were, they might have found a way to give their babies a better start in life.

### *Shirley*

She wanted a boy. That's the first place she looked. She wanted to know if I was a boy or girl. She wanted a boy; she's crying.

She just didn't want to hold me. A man came in; he held

me. He's smiling; he seems happy. She didn't want me by her on the bed. He starts laying me down. She said "no," and he put me in a crib. [She said] "No . . . I don't want her here." I feel hurt. And I'm hungry.

He got angry at her, left the room and slammed the door. She cried and cried. I felt sorry for her. I'm hungry; I start crying. The man came back with another lady . . . She had milk and fed me; she nursed me. I felt warm and snuggly. She fed me lots of times . . . She put me back in the crib and I'd sleep.

### Glenda

Nurse [is holding me]. Now doctor. I'm a fine girl, a real fine girl, the doctor says. I'm here! It's good to be here, good to be out! The doctor is happy too; everybody seems happy.

[My mother] says, "I can't hold it." I'm not an "it"! I'm a beautiful girl! *(Beginning to sob)* She still doesn't want me. She doesn't love me. She hates me . . . She told me. And she doesn't want to hold me. *(Still crying)* And I was so happy!

I'm sad. She doesn't love me. She won't hold me. I feel cold and lonesome . . . *(Whispering)* I'll be very quiet; then they won't know I'm here. I'm so sad. I would like to have privacy to be sad.

The atmosphere was strained and silent at David's birth —more like a funeral, he said later. It was very businesslike. He was placed for adoption at birth. No one was happy to see him.

### David

A man's got me by my leg; he's got his hand around my ankle.

Somebody said, "It's a boy" . . . Behind the doctor is

a man who has on a business suit and a hospital gown over top of it, a face mask, and cap.

It's very quiet. There's no joy in this room. I feel like nobody's happy to see me.

The doctor held me by the feet with one hand. It felt good when he put an arm under me to lay me down. It felt like the first indication that someone cared.

My face is being wiped. Now he's checking me over, stuck a finger in my mouth . . .

The whole room is very silent, like there is death in the room. It's not like anything I'd expect a delivery room to be. I thought that everybody would be very pleasant and happy. Instead it's all businesslike. And there's no feeling of happiness in that room at all.

"Small talk" can sometimes take on large meaning. In the cases of Helen and Brenda, what appears to be light conversation between doctor and mother about "keeping" the child weighs heavily on the child's mind.

## Helen

I'm in her room in the hospital. The doctor is there. Tall, thin man; he's talking to her. She doesn't want me. I'm not a boy.

He said he'd take me home if she didn't want me. I'm "a beautiful, healthy baby." If she doesn't want me, and he does, I'd rather be with him.

She's really disappointed. I couldn't help it! My dad will be disappointed when he comes because he always wanted a boy, too; he always talked about it before. He needs some help on the ranch . . .

I don't like being there with my mother . . . The doctor's standing right by the bed. I want to go back to the nurse. I like it better there. The nun doesn't care if I'm a boy or a girl. She loves us all.

### Brenda

My mother is holding me in her bed. The doctor comes in to see her, all busy and bustling.

"You think you'll keep her?" he asks. "I guess we'll have to now, won't we?" she says.

Puzzling. Do you suppose they didn't want me?

The doctor says, "You can't send them back."

He's a fat doctor. He is pinching me, handling me roughly. I'm crying and he doesn't pay any attention. I don't like him; he's a yucky man!

Mother smiles at him. I wonder which side she is on.

The doctor says I'm "all there," and hands me back all ruffled.

## Exposure to Hostility

On arrival, some babies find themselves on a family battle-field where the outcome is far from certain. Baby Sandra has a teen-age mother waging an unsuccessful battle to keep her. The battle dries up the milk supply. Marie's mother, also a teen, screams because her baby is being taken away before she is ready. The baby wishes things were safe. Hellos and goodbyes are jammed together. In Jackie's family, the hostility comes from the father, who is yelling about the cost of the birth. In Faye's family, it's her sisters who are dangerous.

### Sandra

It's mealtime but there's nothing there. No milk. I'm hungry . . . but no milk. I nurse and nurse but there's nothing. I was hurt; Mommy didn't love me enough to have milk for me . . .

All is white except for mom; she's nice and pink,

cuddly, warm, and tender. I'm on her left, held close. She says, "You're a pretty little baby!" She's telling me I have a wrinkled nose and face. She thinks it's pretty. She kisses my fingers and looks at my belly button . . .

It's quiet. She's crying. She wanted Daddy with us too. Mamma's afraid and crying. "I don't know how to take care of a baby. Poor baby!"

Just tears . . . "I don't know how to take care of my baby! [Aunt] Margaret wants her. I don't want Margaret to take my baby; I'll hide."

Mother's afraid of Margaret. Margaret will take me if she can.

"We can't run away. There's nowhere to go and no one to help us!"

It wasn't warm and snuggly anymore. I'm afraid she'll leave me. I don't want her to leave; I want to be snug again. I want to be held again.

Mother says, "They won't win. They can't have my baby, *can't* have my baby. Damn if they will get her! Her name is [going to be] Sandra, not Barbara. I will do as I please!"

I want Mamma. I don't want Mamma to cry. When Mamma cries I am unhappy.

"I want to have her . . ." Mother is hugging me. "We'll make it; it will be hard."

Then the nurse came. I'm very sleepy. The feeding time is over. There was no milk.

### Marie

I don't remember any other babies. It was not a hospital. It was a home for girls that didn't have a husband . . .

My mother was screaming because she didn't want them to take me. I wanted to say something but I couldn't.

I cried. I just cried because I didn't understand. I didn't

understand what was happening. I wanted things to stay safe and warm. I wanted them to put me back where they got me.

In the delivery room I think I heard my mother say, "I love you . . . I want you." I couldn't say anything. I was frustrated because I wanted to say "I understand" or "I love you too" or something like that.

I think she was screaming and crying, "Don't take her yet!" But I couldn't say anything; I didn't know how. I wanted to tell her that it was all right, that I loved her no matter what, and I'd try to see her again. But I never did. I lived with somebody else.

And I wanted to know more about what happened to her but I never did. [Later] they told me a few things about her, but mostly that she was just beautiful and loved music but was too loose with men. They said she was a "slut" and all kinds of bad things. But she wasn't; that's just what they thought.

## Jackie

They brought me in to my mother and she put my clothes on. She got to hold me. My grandmother came and then we went outside.

It was cold. They had me all in blankets.

Then my dad was there. I didn't know what was happening. My dad was mad about the money and the stereo. He said he didn't have enough money for more babies. Why did she have another baby! They couldn't afford it. He didn't want me.

I was confused. He was yelling. It scared me. My mother was holding me real tight.

He said he didn't have enough money. He had to hock the stereo for my mom to get out of the hospital.

### *Faye*

I find this hard to believe! It feels like I'm coming home from the hospital in my mother's arms.

I'm downstairs in our apartment in my grandparents' house. I came home from the hospital in a car. I had just come in the door and my sisters came and looked at me. They said, "Oh, ick! All red and wrinkly. We don't want it."

From the beginning I don't feel welcomed. I feel like an intruder. (I can't ever remember *not* feeling this way.) . . .

Now I'm in a crib and my sisters are leaning over, telling me that they don't want me and I have no right to be here, and that I messed up their whole lives.!

## A Plague of Fear

Birth, a transition time of marvelous complexity, presents all participants with opportunities for fear. Fear in parents or professionals can easily spread to the baby. Birth memory reports given in hypnosis indicate that babies become frightened when things go wrong with blood and oxygen supplies. Babies react with panic when the umbilical cord becomes compressed or gets wound around the neck. They know when they are losing consciousness and fear the outcome.

Some babies express fear they will be squeezed to death, their heads crushed or "pulled off" by a doctor. Others fear the hospital delivery room, needles, or incubators. They fear being left with strangers, being separated from their mothers, and going unfed or unwatched in the nursery.

Baby Thelma was disturbed by conversation between doctors and nurses. She had a problem breathing at birth, and she overheard them saying they were afraid they might "lose her." From this, she decided it was dangerous to be alone. Thirty years later, when she came to me for psychotherapy, this fear was still with her.

In hypnosis, Thelma slowly became aware of the frightening words she overheard about her condition, but she was reluctant to remember them. When she was finally ready to do so, she recalled:

### Thelma

I'm sick. I hurt [in] my chest; I can't breathe good. Just lying there [alone]. I'm scared. I had pneumonia.

There's a nurse. [She's saying] "It's all right." She's looking down at me; she's touching my head. I feel better; I relax . . .

[They say] I'm sick and they're worried. Got to watch it, make sure it doesn't get worse. They're going to leave somebody there. They could lose me. That's what they said.

I'm scared. I don't want to go. I haven't been here very long. I'm little . . .

Like Thelma, Maxine becomes fearful after hearing adult talk, in this case her mother's. Somehow grasping the danger of her mother's bizarre remarks, she takes an instant dislike to her.

### Maxine

Now I'm being born; I didn't like it at all. There was just so much confusion, everybody around. Just wasn't quiet anymore. I guess I haven't had that quietness since! It's all been upheaval.

I guess I shouldn't say this, but I guess I hated my mother. I hated her from the time I was born. Constant talk and confusion. I couldn't please her.

She said to me, "Why are you here? I don't know how to take care of you." I keep hearing her say, "You're no good," and I just don't understand. I didn't do anything wrong.

She said she loved me and yet she talked like this. One minute she would be nice and another she wouldn't. She was very emotional.

The nurse was there, and she liked me. And my daddy liked me, I could tell. My brother even liked that I had come. He came in to look at me and brought some other children in to see me.

Dr. T. was nice . . . I liked him too.

But I wasn't accepted by my mother.

When I was born my mother said I was a boy! Everybody said I was a girl . . . Then when my father came in, my mother told him I was a boy. I didn't know what to think; it was too confusing for me.

It was hard for me to adjust to this world . . .

Jack is terrified and objects loudly to the way he is handled in the delivery room, but a deeper fear begins when his mother touches him for the first time. There is something wrong. He senses he is not loved for himself but as a tool to repair a marriage. He dreads the future.

## *Jack*

Lights are too bright in the delivery room. I'm screaming; I'm terrified.

It's cold and I'm definitely aware of being held upside down by my feet. I'm trying to right myself. Dumb shit doctor! Slapping me and hanging me like that!

I feel a very healthy arrogance. When I was born I was beautifully arrogant. I felt a fantastic wisdom when I was held there by my feet, but a frustration that all I could do was scream.

The doctor brings me over, umbilical cord and all.

My mother reaches for me and holds me. But it's touching without touching. I'm being touched but I'm not being touched. Held but not caressed. It was an awareness I had when I first went up against my mother's bosom. It was like, "Here we go; it's going to be a long haul!"

I was supposed to solve their [parents'] problems, bring them together. I was supposed to make life beautiful, and all I did was complicate it.

I was a conversation piece for them.

It was on the way home from the hospital that Judy sensed things were precariously balanced at home. Trouble was waiting there. She knew her mother was worried about the other children in the family.

## *Judy*

It seems really bright and sunny. We have a long drive. I'm in the front seat in my mother's arms.

I don't think she wants to go home. Someone is going to be there; I think relatives . . . There's not going to be any peace and quiet when we get home; I just feel it.

Mother has her hand over her face and is looking out the window. *(Worrying)* I just don't know what is going to happen.

I feel like I better go to sleep. I better not bother anybody; I better be a good baby.

My brother and sister are kind of wild and it's going to be awful. They are not good; I know they are not good. I feel they are going to do something the first chance they get. *(Heavy sighing)*

I just don't want to go home, either. There's going to be trouble and I am just too little [to keep the family at peace].

## Scars from Critical Remarks

As a psychologist who helps people find the source of what is bothering them, I have often witnessed the long-term damage that comes from short-sighted remarks made at birth. While remarks made at any time need to be viewed in a larger context, the words said at one's birth seem to be unusually potent. Critical statements that might be brushed off easily at some other time in life seem to hit like thunderbolts and be engraved in the mind. The result is sickness and suffering needing treatment many years later.

Here is a sampler of remarks made to clients of mine at their birth. All turned out to be damaging to mental or physical health and required therapy decades afterward.

*Doctor to nurses:* "Wow, this looks like a sickly one!"

*Nurse to a parent:* "We'll do the best we can for him, but we can't guarantee anything."

*Doctor to nurses:* "Look at her! We're lucky she was born at all, with all of these things wrong!"

*Nurse to nurse:* "Another girl; she's skinny."

*Father to nurse:* "She's not important; take care of the mother."

*Mother to hospital roommate:* "Look at her hairy ears."

*Mother anxiously to doctor:* "What's wrong with her head?"

*Mother to doctor:* "Why didn't you just wrap the umbilical cord around her neck and strangle her?" (Not surprisingly, this daughter said she had "hated her mother from Day One.")

### Ida

They thought I was an ugly baby. All the relatives would comment on it. They were outspoken. They used to make fun of my eyes because they stared. They said I used to look like a frog because I would hold them open real big like I was afraid.

The experience of Baby Stewart gives us an inside look at the way negative suggestions can be generated during labor and delivery. As delivery became more and more difficult, the doctor resorted to name-calling, blame, sarcasm, and ridicule. Uttered during a period of life-threatening danger and distress, his words had a powerful impact on Stewart.

## Stewart

I'm stuck! I can't move my shoulders. The doctor is pulling my head.

My jaws hurt; he's squeezing them, pulling them. Oh, my mouth! He's pulling them harder and harder. The pulling is hurting more and more . . .

It hurts, hurts . . . I feel so tight around my shoulders and the doctor is pulling and I can't get out!

He's yelling at me and pulling. "Push!" he's yelling . . . "Push! Push!"

Things are becoming numb.

He's pulling on my right shoulder trying to get my arm out. He's using his hands and just kind of grabbing to pull me out.

I feel that numbness all over. I feel like my bones are going to break, it's so tight!

The opening is as big as it will go and my mom's crying and pushing. She's not relaxed at all. She's tight and I'm tight and the doctor is really becoming *angry* because I'm not coming out like I'm supposed to.

And he's pulling at my right shoulder harder and harder. I feel caught! Then he pulls on my head. He grabs me around the jaw and the back of my neck and pulls me back and forth, kind of wiggling, pulling one side and then the other trying to get one shoulder out first.

He's trying to hurry. He says I need to breathe soon. I guess that's why he's pulling so hard on my head and right arm. He's rough!

His words are coarse, not gentle at all. He's frustrated because I'm not dropping and I'm not responding; I'm not being a normal child, not doing what I'm supposed to do.

I'm not sure what I'm supposed to do!

He says, "Mrs. E., you have a stubborn child; he's not being quite normal like regular children. They're supposed to drop their hands, and he's not. He's hanging on and I'm trying to pull him down and he's fighting me, I don't know why . . ."

He's not saying very nice things about me. He says I gave him trouble, I was difficult. He was saying to mother that I was going to be a difficult kid. I'm not. I'm not going to be difficult, but he said I was.

Well, it was a silly thing he said about me, but everybody was in agreement; nobody was taking my side. I wanted to say, "No, I'm not!" but they wouldn't listen.

He called me a little fart! He said, "Probably the little fart will be late for everything!" and he laughed like it was a joke. Everybody laughed . . .

I didn't know what was going on but he said it was all my fault—those words are *so* clear!

My desire to say something was strong but I couldn't. I couldn't say anything; I didn't know how. But I wanted to. Everybody was laughing and making me feel bad.

# PART THREE

*Birth:
The Inside Story*

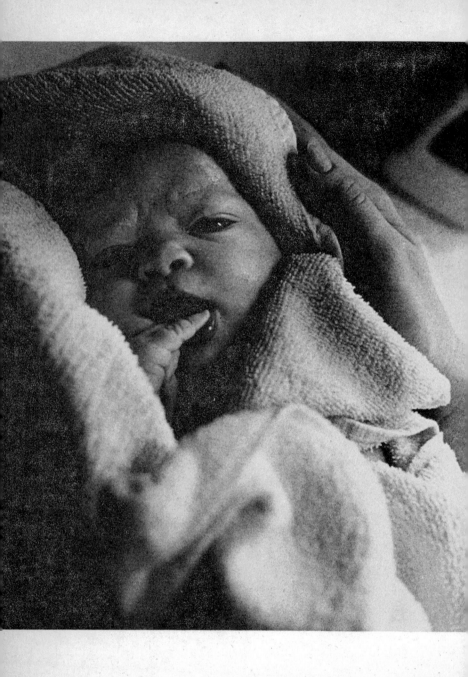

## CHAPTER 11

# Deborah Knew She Had a Mind

$A$ll birth reports reveal an active mind at work, but few contain such forthright declarations and manifestations of mind as this one by Deborah.

When only halfway out of her mother's body, Deborah begins a series of sharp observations. The doctor has his attention elsewhere; a nurse looking after her mother is the first to notice that the baby has arrived. Because her fingers are blue, the staff is slightly flustered and Deborah is passed around, pulled, pushed, and rubbed in a manner she considers unnecessary. She feels a deep certainty that she is all right and tries to communicate this, but nobody is listening. When her most strenuous efforts to communicate are ignored, Deborah becomes angry and wants to "punch somebody."

Sensitive to her mother's state of mind, Deborah notes that her mother tries to see what is going on but is pushed back down on the table. Deborah wants her mother to know she is all right, just cold. Later, she notes that her mother still looks worried, is not sure if everything is all right, and is crying a little, "but not like before."

A ringing declaration of infant intelligence ends the report, as Deborah compares her knowledge with that of the hospital staff. Saying that she was more aware of being a mind than a person, she speaks of feeling intelligent and explains why. She decided she was more intelligent than those caring for her, because she knew the real situation *inside* while they seemed to know only the outside. She was also superior in being able to receive their messages while they were unable to receive hers.

### *Watch Out, Here I Come!*

The doctor is looking around for something.

I'm coming out, but just my eyes, I think. My body feels warm and closed in, but my head's starting to feel cold, and I see all these people and the bright yellow room.

The doctor has black hair and a white coat and he's looking at a tray of instruments. He's turned away from me. I don't think he knows I'm coming out.

Somebody better tell him I'm going to come out! I think I'm just going to do it by myself. He'll turn around and I'll just be there. I don't know what he's looking for; it sure seems important.

One of the nurses is watching my mother, and then she notices that I'm there. She has yellow hair and a white dress and a white hat.

I feel cold all over and squirmy. I don't feel comfortable. A bunch of people are grabbing at me like they can't decide who's supposed to take me. I don't want anybody to take me.

I don't think I like this very much. I think I want to go back inside. I don't like all these people, these hands. They're pulling on me. I think they are having trouble getting the rest of me out.

I'm out but there's part of me left in there, the rest of the cord and all that stuff. They keep handing me back and forth from the doctor to nurse. I wish they'd make up their minds who's supposed to get me. They're kind of pushing and pulling on me. They're mashing me around.

## The Wrong Color

I feel awful cold all over, especially my hands and feet. I think I'm not supposed to be this cold. My mom's trying to look around and see what's going on. They keep pushing her back down on the table. She's starting to cry because she doesn't know what's happening, and she thinks something is the matter with me.

I'm all right. I'm just cold. I'm just wanting these people to leave me alone, and they're still mashing on me. They're pulling on my hands and feet, kind of rubbing on them real hard. Why don't they just leave me alone? I'm all right, really I am. Just leave me alone.

Everybody's all around, pulling on my fingers and rubbing them. I guess they think I'm the wrong color . . . that's what it is—my fingers are blue. That's why they are so cold. They put me by somebody now, on a blanket, lots of blankets. Somebody's holding me. It's the nurse with the yellow hair. I'm all wrapped up real tight now. I can't wiggle around anymore but at least they quit mashing me.

Now she's smiling at me. And she's showing my mom that I'm okay. But I'm still all wrapped up so my mother can't see very much of me except my face. She still looks worried. My mom's still not sure.

They let her hold me for a little while. My hands are still cold, wrapped up. Mom's still crying a little bit but not like she was before. Everything's okay now, so I can go to sleep.

## Nobody Was Listening

I knew I was okay. I tried to tell everybody, but they wouldn't listen. I was trying to talk but they didn't understand me. And I was trying to push them away with my hands, but there were too many of them. I was crying, trying to talk, but I guess it was just crying to them.

## How It Was Inside

Inside [the womb] it was quiet and warm and comfortable. Dark. Nobody to bother me. I was very happy with the way it was. Then it all happened pretty fast. Everything was quiet and just fine, when all of a sudden I knew something was going on.

There was a lot of rumbling and moving up and down. I was not exactly scared, just really surprised. I hadn't done anything; I was just lying there. But something was happening and I knew there wasn't a whole lot I could do about it. At first I didn't think it had anything to do with me. I figured I would just wait and pretty soon it would go away.

It had happened once before but it didn't last very long, just a short while. That's why I figured if I just stayed still it would stop again like it did before; that it didn't have anything to do with me—it was something on the outside. But then I knew this time was different because it kept going, and it got worse.

## Labor Got Serious

I was getting all pushed around and shook up. I had a feeling something was going to happen that I wasn't going to like. I figured any change wasn't going to be too good because I liked things just the way they were and I didn't want to change them. They were being changed without me.

I didn't want to have to go along with it, but I had a feeling I was going to anyway. I still kept hoping it was going to stop, and yet knowing deep down that it wasn't going to. But I still had no idea what it would end up like, what all the shaking and everything was going to lead to.

## Life Outside the Womb

Then all of a sudden there was this yellow room and these people. That's when I was beginning to figure out what was going on. Not very happy about it. I guess I started telling them right off what I thought about it!

At first I was just making a lot of faces. Trying to look real mean, because I couldn't get my hands free right away. What I felt like doing was shaking my fists, but they were still stuck. So about all I could do was make faces, because I didn't realize right off that I could make noises—that seemed to just kind of happen.

When I was by myself [inside] there was no need for noise. And I liked it that way. I guess I was pretty mad about the whole thing, but I wasn't quite sure who to be mad at, just mad generally, I guess, for being disturbed.

Just as soon as I got my arms loose, I shook 'em around. I felt like punching somebody! I guess I was waving around pretty good. That was when they noticed that my hands were blue. But I was too busy to notice. Besides, I didn't know what blue hands were. I just knew I was pretty mad, and it was about that time I figured out I could make noises. I just got so mad with the situation, something came out.

It sort of surprised me but it didn't seem to surprise them too much. They didn't take much notice at all. I was not only mad, I was getting frustrated, too, because there wasn't anything I could do. I wanted to thrash around and punch somebody, and everybody was holding me down—all these hands holding me down and mashing and rubbing and grabbing. So I just made a lot of noise, because that seemed to be about the only thing I could do.

## Breathing and Making Noise

Starting to breathe was pretty strange, too. I had never done anything like that before. I'd always just lain around and listened to the quiet, feeling warm. [Breathing] was another surprise like the noise. It was like a little explosion. When the noise came there was the air. But that was a good thing because the air made the noise louder. The more air there was, the louder the noise. That was a good idea because I was trying to get their attention.

The breathing was just in bursts at first, every time I made a noise. Then I noticed every time I was doing it I was doing it in between the noises, so I was thinking about that, too. It kind of distracted me from being mad because I was concentrating on what was going on inside me. Listening to the way it sounded. Feeling the air go in and out. Making it go faster and slower—that was kind of a neat idea. I thought as long as I had to be in this place, I might as well have something like noise and air. Kind of gave me something to do.

## A Big Change

One of the things that really made me mad about the whole situation is this: All the time I was in there by myself, everything was just how I wanted it. And I figured that was it. I sort of had a feeling there were other things around but not people, not people like me. But they didn't really matter because they were outside.

Then when I came out, it made me mad because I didn't have anything to say about it. When I tried to, nobody paid any attention to me. That made me mad, too, because I always thought I knew what was going on.

## An Intelligent Mind

I felt I knew a lot—I really did. I thought I was pretty intelligent. I never thought about being a person, just a mind. I thought I was an intelligent mind. And so when the situation was forced on me, I didn't like it too much.

I saw all these people acting real crazy. That's when I thought I really had a *more* intelligent mind, because I knew what the situation was with me, and they didn't seem to.

They seemed to ignore me. They were doing things *to* me—to the *outside* of me. But they acted like that's all there was. When I tried to tell them things, they just wouldn't listen, like that noise wasn't really anything. It didn't sound too impressive, but it was all I had.

I just really felt like I was more intelligent than they were.

## CHAPTER 12

# Kit Faces Death at Birth

**K**it opens a magic window through which we can see not only the dramatic details of an unusual birth but also the astute mixture of feelings and thoughts that were pouring through her at the time. Like many others who remember birth, she has a double perspective: she is a participant-observer. She is profoundly and painfully aware of her physical body but this does not impair the operation of her mind. Displaying a wisdom for which we are in no way prepared, she recites the facts, examines possibilities, plumbs the character of the nurse and doctor, and faces moral dilemmas alone. She illustrates for us the strong bond of affectionate concern which is often shown between baby and mother in birth reports.

At various times in her thirty-seven years, Kit had suffered from a mysterious breathing problem involving a heavy feeling in her chest and the inability to get enough oxygen into her system. As we began to explore this set of feelings in hypnosis, Kit suddenly experienced great emotion, began to gasp and cry, and remembered that she almost suffocated at birth. What follows are excerpts from Kit's story.

Rarely, in modern times, is the life of a mother and child at risk in childbirth, but in this case valiant efforts were required of their medical team. Kit describes in detail the procedure used to save her life, appreciates the dialog between nurse and doctor, and even sets their opinions in a larger context of knowledge including her own sphere of inside knowledge.

The nurse wants to give up and go home because they've been there too long and she fears the child's brain is hopelessly damaged. The doctor, showing fierce determination, tries out various tubes and struggles through a procedure he has never done before. While this is going on, Kit transmits information from the scene: "I'm getting stiff . . . numb . . . it's not helping."

This suggests the possibility of a visionary obstetrics where doctors actually receive feedback from babies and the two collaborate in meeting emergencies at birth. While the physician was trying to get a tube into her lungs, she tells us "It's down too far . . . it's all the way down in my stomach!" Later, when a larger tube is correctly inserted, she says "I'm getting a little bit but it still isn't enough. If he could just get it down a little bit deeper." She comments that people don't understand that babies can *communicate* and that they don't need words to do this.

Throughout the ordeal, Kit's thoughts and concerns continually turn back to her mother. Still in the womb, Kit is aware that a grave condition has developed, and she faces a lonely decision on a matter of life and death. It seems she is the first to know about an internal hemorrhage and is trying to stem the flow with her body. If she turns herself, as she must do for birth, the situation will become critical. She doesn't want to die and doesn't want her mother to die. If her mother does die, Kit wants "to die too and be where she was."

## An Emergency in the Womb

*(Moaning)* There's too much blood all over. Nobody knows it yet. She [mother] is completely filled with it and I'm the only one keeping it from coming out! *(Sobs)*

Ohhh . . . If I come out and she dies, she'll never know how much I love her! I want to know her. She talked to me a lot before I was born but nobody else knew because they'd think she was silly.

I think they ought to just go ahead and let me die. I feel like she's had enough suffering. *(Gasps and sobs)* I didn't sense it [her suffering] until she started filling up with blood. *(Sharp sobs)*

I felt like I was going to drown, and I knew I wasn't supposed to. *(Sobs)* I don't know what I should do!

Oh, God, I don't want to drown in blood! I'm afraid I'm going to. *(Sobs)* I don't want *her* to die, either. If I don't come out, they're going to grab me. Ohhh, they just don't understand what's happening!

Ohhh, I'm out now, and I can see it [blood]; it's everywhere! And she [mother] looks so helpless. I wish I could have done something.

If I had a chance, I would have talked to her. I would have told her that everything was going to be okay. They don't understand that babies can do that. We don't have to say words all the time.

They were holding me upside down and they keep hitting me. I don't like to be hit. I can't really feel it but I don't like it anyway. If they'd just let my mother have me, we'd be okay. They're cleaning my mother up now, and they're putting blood in her. She's trying to talk to my father, to reassure him. Ohhh, ohhh, I wish they'd figure out something for me! I'm completely numb now. I'm stiff. The nurse wants the doctor to just stop because she thinks I'm dead. The doctor just told her to shut up . . . they're not going to stop.

### The Doctor Will Not Give Up

I wish they'd hurry up! I'm stiff as a board. *(Gasping)* He wants to stick a tube down my throat, but I don't want him to. Ohhhh, it's going to make me sick! *(Gasps)* It's not helping! He's stuffing it all the way down me. It's awful! Ohhhh, it feels as if they've pushed it down too far. It's all the way down in my stomach. *(Heavy sighs, gasping)* The doctor's got me cradled in his arms. And the reason he's got the tube pushed down too far is that he's never done this before. It's a new procedure. There's nothing I can do.

He's got the tube in his mouth now. He's telling everyone to get away from him and leave him alone. They think he's kind of nuts. He knows that this is the last chance because I've been without oxygen much too long! He's holding me because he can feel I'm stiff. Ohhhh, my hands hurt, they're so numb! He has the tube in his mouth but it's not big enough. So he's just pulled it out, frantically, and he's yelling at someone.

He wants a big tube. He wants the biggest one they can safely fit down my throat. They just brought another one and he's mad at the nurse because she's taking so long. He sees a great big one over there and he yells to her to grab it quick. It's attached to something else but he grabs it and pushes it down inside of me as fast as he can until it goes as far as it can and he yells for scissors, fast. Ohhhh! *(Gasping)* He cuts it real quick, cuts it short so it barely sticks out of my mouth. He's pushing my head back and puts his mouth over my whole face practically. *(Gasping)* I'm getting a little bit but it still isn't enough. *(Repeated gasps)* If he could just get it down a little bit deeper!

Oh, it's been so long! I can't feel anything except the upper part of my chest. [The rest] feels dead and numb. And it feels like my body's shriveling up. That's why the nurse keeps saying, "She's dead." She wants to go home. They've been there all night. He's pushing on my stomach, too. I wish I could straighten out my hand; it hurts. If they don't hurry up, I'm going to be in real trouble. The nurse said even if they get me breathing now, I won't be okay; she said it's been much too long.

I know if they'll get me breathing I'll be just fine. But [the nurse] knows that I haven't breathed for so long that my brain will be dead—that's what she thinks. But I know she's wrong. She'd never seen this done before.

*(Gasping)* I can tell he [the doctor] really wants to help me. He's pulling the tube out of me and I don't like the way it feels; it's making me feel sick. And he's rubbing my chest with his fingers now. *(Hard breathing, sighing)* I'm breathing by myself now, but it's hard. We're all starting to feel better now. I feel like crying and I'm not sure why . . .

## Will She See Mother Again?

Ohhh! They just said *I'm* going to die too. There's not enough blood for my mother. They keep squashing me. *(Gasping)*

. . . She's okay now, but I can't breathe. I still wish I knew where she was.

I can see her now. She's trying to reach for me. She's too weak, and I still can't breathe. I want to but I still can't. *(Gasps)* I'm trying, but it just doesn't seem to be right. It doesn't feel like the air is getting down deep enough. I can feel the air going in but it doesn't feel right. I'm getting really numb.

Somebody just hit me [on] my bottom. They hit kind of hard . . .

I need to be put with my mother, but they put me in a room by myself. I was very confused. I wasn't sure if I'd ever see my mother again. I thought she must have died after all and that's why they put me in this room until they figured out what they were going to do with me.

## Is Mother All Right?

I don't know why I'm crying! *(Sobbing and shaking)* I just feel scared and sad and I don't know why. I'm thinking about my mommy. I don't want her to die! *(Sharp cry)* I can't see her! I don't know where she is. *(Sobbing)* Ooohhh . . . I think my mommy's dying! I don't want to live if she's dying! I'm scared.

They're cutting her. There's lots of blood. *(Moaning, teeth chattering)* She's bleeding to death! I just know it.

*(Sobbing)* I can't breathe. I don't care; I don't want to breathe anyway. I don't like it here at all; it's scaring me! I feel kind of numb. *(Heavy sighing)*

They're trying to make me breathe. I wish they'd stop it. They're squashing me. They're forcing me to breathe. It's not working! Ohhh, I'm getting numb. I want to know where my mommy is! *(Agonizing sobs)*

It's all my fault! I just know it is . . . *(Teeth chattering, moaning)* That's why I didn't want to come out, because I knew it was going to be trouble. I didn't want to hurt her. That's why I wouldn't turn around. *(Spoken in a childish whine, and sobbing)* They were going to make me come out, so I had to!

I don't know where my mommy is! Ohhh, I can't breathe. I'm not going to breathe until she's okay!

*(Sighing)* I felt that if my mommy was dead, then I wanted to die too and be where she was. All I could think about was that I wanted to die. And I felt completely alone. I couldn't understand why they were leaving me alone, because there was nothing the matter with me.

I felt real bad because before I was born my mother told me that I was going to be very special. She knew I was going to be a girl. That's why I knew the nurse was wrong. I knew if I could start breathing, I'd be okay.

They never put me with my mother the whole time I was there . . .

Today Kit is an active business executive with a keen mind and beautiful personality. Her relationship with her mother has always been warm and loving.

## CHAPTER 13

# *Jeffrey—The Meaning of Touch*

*J*effrey illustrates zest for living as he provides us with exquisite descriptions of his first experiences outside the womb. From the breaking of the water sac in labor to his arrival in the arms of his mother, he tells all. He is expert in interpreting the many meanings of touch and lets us see that touch is both fearful and wonderful; skin sensations bring excitement, reassurance, and bliss. His new experiences are interesting but they play against a background of continuing fear.

What fun it is to use his eyes, ears, and muscles! He sees pictures when he sleeps. Hunger pangs are new, and bottles are new, but he knows what to do.

He perceives something magical in the touch and presence of his mother, and senses her pride as she speaks his name over and over "for her own satisfaction." When she speaks to him, it feels good. He knows he "has nothing to worry about with this person." He senses that his mother, different from all the others who are caring for him, cares *totally*.

## Contented and Waiting

Darkness. There is warmth all around me. There's a feeling of anticipation, as if I know something is going to happen. It's a new feeling. Things push at me from all sides. I'm waiting for something I know will make me happy. Darkness . . . and a sense of contentment—that seems to be the undercurrent of my emotions.

I hear a separate heartbeat. I'm aware that the sounds I hear are not *my* sounds. There is movement all around me. The things that surround me keep pushing at me.

## Labor Begins

[After the amniotic sac breaks] my skin feels different. Something is missing, something around me is gone. It's still warm but in a different way. Next I notice my position is changed. I feel myself being pulled down onto my head, as if my head were on the bottom. Something is holding me very, very tight and pushing me, pushing me all the while. There is fear, much fear!

Movement, strange movement—not what I was used to. Lots of movement. It's warmer, hot. There is something moving me. It's everywhere. I turn and it is still there. The fear goes away.

There is a sense of waiting, as if I know something is about to happen. Something around me again. It's moving. The fear comes back, much fear! So many things happening! I'm not where I was, I can tell.

It's all around me. I feel it sliding past me. I feel constricted, squeezed in. Much fear! It's not quiet anymore, not still and peaceful. The noises—loud noises, air, liquid kind of noise. I feel whatever is rubbing past me is making a terrible loud noise. Something else touches me. It feels good. It's touching . . . it's the doctor, I guess. I can feel the shape; I feel hands. There is still a lot of fear, but the hands feel good. Much fear and pain!

## Suddenly, Born!

Everything happens at once. Then suddenly there is nothing. My skin feels so strange! A wash of cool air comes across me and excites me momentarily. The fear is always there while this is happening. Fear is the dominant emotion.

There are so many things going on that have never happened before. Everything before has been constant, always the same. Now everything is different.

Suddenly there is something else I don't understand. I see light! I don't understand what it is. I'm afraid. I can move. I can move all I want and nothing stops me. Still, I don't know what has happened . . . I'm afraid.

I heard different voices. A man's voice says, "It's okay; it's okay!"—a very loud voice. I heard other voices. I heard a voice different from the others. It was not trying to say anything . . . just a noise. I could feel a sense of pain with the noise. There was something special about that voice. Suddenly there is much pain. I scream! I can feel myself breathing. I feel the tightness in my throat. The more I scream the tighter it gets. I want to stop it but it just makes me scream more.

## Calmed by Human Touch

When someone holds me it feels good; for some reason I don't have to scream. I don't like to be afraid. Before when everything was dark, I always knew everything was all right, even with the fear. Now the fear seems to be stronger.

Someone is holding me now. It feels so good to have something around me. I can close my eyes and everything is like it was before. I don't know who is holding me. I can't see faces, just shapes. I don't know what anything is. I see the shapes of people. There is light everywhere. Even when I close my eyes it's lighter than before. There's discovery, excitement. And still a lot of fear. I am afraid most of the time, but some of the things feel so good!

Looking at things using my eyes is so much fun. The more I do it the more fun it is. I love to see things move. I feel movement now; I feel bouncing up and down.

Someone is holding me; they must be walking some-where. I like it when they touch me. Feels good; it's an-other new thing. When they touch me it is warm, reassuring.

## Inside the Incubator

I see something shiny around me. The light reflects off of it. It's glass or Plexiglas around me. When I move now it's different, something pushing against my back in different spots. When I move my head the lights and the colors change, the shapes change. At first it is scary—nothing moved before. Whatever I do, there is always something beneath me, something solid—it's one of the first things I was aware of.

It feels good. I move and it's there. I want to do so many things! I want to move but I don't know how to move the way I want to. It feels so different to move now. My hands and legs move so easily—all I can think of is to move them. There is no purpose but just to feel them move. I'm very awkward at it.

So many sounds! They are much louder. Sometimes I want them to go away. There are good sounds, too. Good sounds come when someone holds me. I want someone to hold me. It feels good to be touched. They don't hold me enough. I want to feel close again, feel surrounded.

There are so many things, and no way to form them in my head. I want more pictures but I don't know how to get them. I just want pictures, as if the more pictures I have, the better I feel. I feel empty without pictures. I want to *make* pictures, but they just happen. I want to *make* things move, but they don't. I reach out and there's noth-ing. I want to see things move. I can watch myself move; my arms move in front of my face. I am always lying on my back. I still see the box. It's hard to see out of the box.

### Sleep and Dreams

I like to sleep because when I close my eyes and the light goes away, the pictures come, pictures of things I've seen. Only I don't see them just the way they happened. I see shiny metal things that are intriguing. I see pictures and I want to touch them. I want to know what the shiny feels like. I reach out and they aren't there! In the box there are frustrations but there are still discoveries.

I'm still discovering and testing. Discovering myself. Parts of me move when I want them to, and they don't when I don't want them to. Everything is so new! I discover the same things many times. My arms and legs—I keep moving them, and each time it is like the first time.

### Getting Hungry

I got hungry. It was a feeling I had never had before. I knew it was not good. It was uncomfortable, painful, and I tried to communicate that something was wrong. Every time I did this someone would pick me up and hold me. There were times when that wasn't enough. I'd want something to eat and I'd keep on crying. It took me some time to connect eating with feeling good, or eating and this feeling [hunger] going away. Perhaps it was two or three times before I knew that eating would get rid of it.

It was always warm and satisfying to drink. After I learned the experience it became very enjoyable, something I looked forward to. The first time it happened someone was holding me. I think probably it was a woman. She held something [a bottle] to my lips and I automatically started sucking, drawing something in. The milk came and I swallowed. I knew what to do.

## The Magic of Mother

I see the hospital room. It seems later, perhaps a day later. It stands out that this is the first time I knew the difference between anyone who held me. This time, when she [mother] held me, I could tell that she was a different person—someone special. Somehow I just knew that I was safe with her, that I had nothing to worry about with this person.

She repeated my name several times proudly, as if to say, "This is my son." She was just repeating my name for her own satisfaction. When she spoke to me or about me, it made me feel good. When she held me or spoke to me, there was just something different. I could tell she cared for me in a way the others didn't. The others were concerned but she was totally concerned. With the others I was just a part of the job. With her I was her only thought —that's the feeling I got.

She is holding me now. I see her holding a bottle. This person is concerned about me. This person has nothing but me on her mind.

## CHAPTER 14

# Kristina Is Loved by Her Parents

**K**ristina was the first child of immigrant parents from Sweden, born in a hospital in the Bronx. Her mother primarily spoke Swedish, so communication with birth helpers was awkward—but this didn't bother Kris. Like other babies, she seems to understand both languages and to comprehend her mother's emotional outbursts. When father comes on the scene she has no difficulty understanding the language of his pride, excitement, and affection for his American baby.

All memories of birth are not happy, but I would put this one at the top of the happy list. At nearly sixty, Kris was very surprised to have this memory; she didn't think she had it in her. She was also surprised to discover her parents so deliriously happy, something rarely seen in succeeding years. Perhaps most important of all, Kris was reunited with a rare feeling of perfection in herself. "I'm the prize!" she said. "I have never felt so perfect, so marvelous!"

### Being Born

I'm looking at the floor; my head is down. My shoulder's up, like stuck. Oh gosh, strange! It's cold. Oh, my God! This is really weird. It's like . . . somebody has a hand on my waist. I'm so tiny . . . just a little tiny thing about six or seven pounds. I'm right there looking . . .

I'm down, coming out, but somebody is grabbing me, working my shoulder through. This one is out. *(She moves shoulder)* My head is out. My head is facing down. They're working around it *(other shoulder).* There's a big cord hanging there. My little leg's kind of bent. I'm out! Golly, what a mess!

My mother is screaming, like a "Whoopie!" scream. It's over!

My mother . . . it's like saying good-bye to her. It was nice and warm in there. I don't understand at all. It's really exciting.

I see walls and a lot of windows, big windows. It's like it's daylight. I can see it so clear. There are a lot of window panes. Oh, it's so light in that room!

I'm just hanging there like this . . . and this ugly cord is going in somewhere. I'm a mess; I feel all sweaty and dirty. Yuck! And I feel really excited.

There is a lot of noise, a lot of people screaming. It's the strangest thing because they all have accents like they live in the Bronx, and that's where this is taking place. Someone is saying, "Put her down, put her down, it's okay."

Oh, I'm screaming, you know, "Whaaaaa" . . . real loud. Here I am, world! That's the strangest thing. Wow! Who is supposed to know about anything like that? I never even thought about it in my whole life. There is nothing wrong with me, I can tell you that.

It's weird, strange. I can feel it, though; I can feel it happening to me. I'm getting kind of lonely for my mother. I'm lying someplace, in some kind of little box. I'm still screaming—a very happy scream. I can see my face. I have hair, kind of curly and blond in the back. I'm very new, brand new. And I want to go back to my mother, like right *now.*

I'm waiting and those people are walking around me. It's okay. The sun is shining and I want to go see my mother, get up close. I know I'm supposed to have something close to me right now, like I'm supposed to come out of the birth canal and just climb right up and hang on to the source of all the comfort, my mother. And she's just lying there breathing a lot. She's all worn out. She really wants to get a hold of me, too. She waited seven years to have me.

I'm just lying there, kicking out my heels. I'm screaming, having a fine old time. "Take me where I'm supposed to go!" I'm not bashful, just like a tiny little animal.

A nurse is coming by. She has a little white plain cap, like from a city hospital, a white starchy uniform . . . a very buxom lady. Ha! A very funny-looking gal. I think she is going to pick me up.

Now I feel like I'm wrapped up in something, a blanket, a white receiving blanket; that's all I have on me. And people are clucking a lot—cluck, cluck, cluck—nice sounds. I really don't care. I need to go somewhere. I feel very separated.

And my mother is just lying over there on the table. She is breathing a lot and she is relieved and she's asking for me now. She has trouble with her English. She's trying hard.

## Getting Back in Touch with Mother

Somebody's picking me up; it's the buxom lady with the little hat. There she is, picking me up, and I'm starting to feel a little cozy. I can see my mother. She's got her arms out. Now she is holding me. Oh, my! That is the ultimate! She's really happy. That's so strange! I'm just all cuddled up like a brand-new baby, and that's the way it is supposed to be.

My mother is talking and saying things. I don't know what she is saying but I know what she wants. I feel that she wants . . . my father to come and see me. She's telling somebody she wants to see my father. She's just thrilled!

I never saw my mother so thrilled. She's just happy, happy, happy.

I'm lying there like a little chipmunk chirping away, really happy. Everything's wonderful. It's a nice world. Except my father has to come and see me. Oh, my goodness! How could I be thinking things like this?

I'm just lying there wrapped up and she's tugging at me, looking at my fuzzy hair. She's very satisfied. And she is speaking Swedish, too, billing and cooing over me. She's really proud of herself. And I feel very wet and slimy but it doesn't matter.

There's the lady with the large bosom. She is trying to talk to my mother. Just more clucking . . . my, how satisfied we are! She's standing on the left and I'm lying on the left. Everybody is sort of mopping up and clunking away with the tools on the tray.

Now they are going to take me away somewhere. I'm not too happy about that. The nurse is reaching over. I don't want to leave, but I just can't believe this. Oh dear, this is really strange! I'm so comfortable and warm. And my mother is stroking my little head. She doesn't want me to go, either. I think I'm feeling the vibrations of how happy she is. She's scared, though, I can tell. She speaks Swedish all the time, saying she has to learn English, but she gets nervous in a situation like this. She's just trying to figure it all out.

All I know is that I'm lying there just as happy as a bedbug. I don't understand this at all . . . but I'm still feeling it! Just one of God's little children. Just perfect. Just can hardly wait to get on with whatever. It's such a miracle!

It's very hard for me to believe that I'm going through this right now. It's absolutely the most fascinating thing in the world. I actually *feel* like this perfect little tiny baby. I see myself lying there quietly someplace. And now I'm going to sleep.

## Excitement about Father's Arrival

I see my father. He's so young! Oh, no, I can't believe this. He's got hair! I never saw him like that before. There's his hair; he didn't lose it yet—oh, that is the strangest thing!

He's got a white shirt on and he's so happy, standing there playing with my feet. He's kind of cute; he's big. And there's my mother showing me off to him. My mother has just really outdone herself! "Isn't she cute!" But she's saying it in Swedish, and it comes out so soft.

My father is very agreeable; he's smiling and he's picking me up now. More words are spoken in Swedish. Well, no wonder I'm all puffed up, so pleased with myself. And he's shaking my little fists around and I . . . feel so loved. I feel so wanted and loved. It isn't going to last very long, I know that.


## Feeling Perfect

I'm like a little cream puff and I can *feel* the vibrations. They waited seven years to have me. If they were disappointed that I wasn't a boy, they didn't show it. No, no, they're just standing there like two silly little kids. And I'm the prize.

And I just know it, too. I'm just so little and so perfect and so loved! And I don't even know how to talk—all I can do is scream and holler and carry on. My little legs are just going up and down. I'm just having a wonderful time.

I have no idea why, but I'm getting a tremendous reception. I've never even seen my parents look so happy and delighted. My mother is absolutely beside herself.

She can't get enough of me, and of course they are going to take me away from her now. She's not too happy about that. My father says, that's the way it goes. This is wonderful America and it's going to be better for me—

this is what I'm feeling. I don't understand any of this, but it's absolutely fantastic.

I have never felt so perfect, so marvelous! Ten little fingers, ten little toes, little squawker squawking away. Everything's working. A deluxe model—not a thing wrong! Gee, it's wonderful to be so perfect, to be such a source of pleasure, to see what I'm seeing here, to see my mother. And there is my father with his little American baby. There she is, just as perfect as can be—the little Olson girl.

## CHAPTER 15

# Charles's World Is Changed

Charles provides us with a distinctive moment-by-moment account of the journey through the birth canal. New sensations are compared with old. Charles discovered after birth that he was part of a medical emergency; his mother was bleeding and might die. In the midst of crisis, he is struck that the doctor refers to him as a bastard and wonders if he is to blame for his mother's trouble. Before he can learn for sure if she is alive or dead, he is wheeled from the scene, those caring for him oblivious to his need to be with her or to be reassured of her safety. They have no idea what he has on his mind.

He speaks for many when he tells us how much his world has changed in moving from a womb of constant touching to a cold delivery room where he is set apart. Another common theme is that reunion with mother is like joining the world again. Unfortunately, he is already wondering whom to trust and where he really belongs.

## Journey down the Birth Canal

I hear noises like sounds your stomach makes. And there's a long tunnel in front of me. I can't even see myself. I see in shadows, not pitch-dark, just a small amount of light. I found myself moving, and then there was a flash of light, but I was still back in the tunnel. There are sounds of different people talking. Muffled noises. I don't think I'm all crunched up now.

I don't see my legs or anything; they're behind me somewhere. I'm lying on my stomach. I don't know if I am moving down the tunnel or if the tunnel is coming to me. It seems to be getting lighter. I picture myself being born, coming out head first, face down. It got light all of a sudden. I feel my body being bent down when my head and shoulders come out.

The doctor, or whoever's got me, is bending me towards my stomach. I guess I come out easier that way. It's cool. People sort of mumbling; I don't understand what they are saying.

## From Womb to Tray

The doctor puts me on a metal tray. It's cold. There are a lot of lights; it's not what I have been used to. All I can see is light; I can't see anybody. I hear noises, stuff being dropped in trays—tools or something—and people mumbling. Nobody touched me after that.

It seemed so cold because I was in a warm place before. When I was coming out, that was the only time I was cold. It felt funny, a new experience. When I was being turned over I was wondering what was happening because I had never been turned over before, either. I'm in this tray about twice as wide as I am. I don't know what's happening and I'm cold.

For the first time I'm lying somewhere and I'm not touching on the sides; the only place I can feel anything is on my back.

## Disturbing Words

I could hear all these noises . . . like they put me aside to take care of my mother. I could hear all these tools and things, yet they weren't doing anything to me. I get the impression that my mother was bleeding.

A doctor said they were working to stop the bleeding. He said she was bleeding real bad and "we have to stop it." They are working real fast, like they don't know if they can stop the bleeding. I get the impression they think my mother is going to die.

They don't think they can help her. I sense that someone said something like, "Why wasn't he born dead; then she wouldn't be in such bad shape!" I had another flash that the doctor said something about a bastard—that I was a bastard. It's not that I'm listening to conversation; they are just messages or flashes that I get, if you know what I mean.

And then I find myself moving. It's not like a nurse picks me up; I'm just in this tray, but it's moving. The impression I have is like being on a stand and the stand is rolling and I'm wondering where we're going. I don't know if they are done with her or if they are still working. I never heard them say if they stopped the bleeding. Everything seemed to be puzzling to me: not understanding what was happening, where I was, why I was cold, why there was light all of a sudden, and why there was always light now.

### Cold and Alone

I'm just lying there taking it all in. I feel alone. I can't hear anybody, can't feel anybody. It's cold and I don't understand what's happening. In a matter of a couple of minutes everything has changed.

I sense that I am getting ready to cry, like I want to scream or make some sound. I was wanting to cry to see if somebody is around, if somebody would come. I don't know why I would do that because I've never done it before; it's like an instinct.

I'm cold all over. There's just no warmth coming from anywhere. I'm crying out loud and somebody comes over.

I feel the warmth just from them being close by; I feel the heat from them.

They don't pick me up. Whoever is there is just rocking the stand or tray, just moving it. I feel better just to know there's somebody there. I stop crying.

The pan keeps moving back and forth and I fall asleep. I don't hear anybody talking. It's like it was routine for the nurse, or whoever, to come over and start rocking. Nobody said anything while I was in that room. The only time I felt someone was around was when the pan started to move.

### In the Nursery: Still No Touching

When I woke up I was someplace else. It's warmer and I can hear babies crying. Some noises sound like I am in the same room. Then there are faraway sounds, maybe in a different room. I have a blanket or something over me. I don't see myself getting picked up or touched. Before I was born I was constantly touched or surrounded. And then after that I'm not being touched . . .

### Back with Mother

I see myself wrapped in a blanket. I'm still in the hospital but I'm on the bed with my mother. She's holding me. She's got the top part of the bed up on an angle and she's sitting up holding me. She is happy. She says I'm a beautiful baby. I'm sort of bewildered, though. There's something I don't understand. Before, I wasn't handled, and now I am.

I just don't understand; there's an uneasiness. I was getting used to not being touched, and I was accepting that. And now she's holding me and cuddling me. Somebody comes in and she has to show me off to them. I guess she's proud of me.

## *Charles Wonders If He Belongs*

I see other people in the room. They're concerned about my mother. I see my uncle and my grandmother. They're relieved that my mother didn't die, and they're upset at her for making the decision to let me be born and taking the extreme chance of dying. It was like they didn't want to lose her. She's arguing back at them—something to the effect that she has lived and she wanted me to live and if she had died then it would have been worth it, as long as I was born all right. They don't look at it that way.

I have an uneasy feeling. I'm wondering, Is this where I belong? I wonder if I should be back in my bed listening to the other kids crying and not being touched—like I'm trying to decide where I'm supposed to be. Then the nurse comes in and takes me back into the other room with the other children.

## CHAPTER 16

# *Elaine: A Baby's Prescription for Birth*

$D$octors are known for their recommendations. What if babies could recommend? What prescription would they write for birth? Elaine gives us an idea. Her wishes are a reflection of what one can find in almost any birth report. She was born about twenty years ago in a medium-size Colorado town but it could have been almost anywhere in the Western world. She tells the worst and best of her experience, with comments on how *she* would have done it if *she* were in charge.

Her brief description of life in a delivery room reads like a catalog of machine-age birth. She begins by being passed from one stranger to another and ends up in an incubator. In between she is exposed to cold scales, a painful needle, held down while a gummy ointment is put into her eyes, footprinted, and handprinted.

Obstetrical routine then creates a chasm separating her from the soothing touch and words of her mother. She speculates about what her mother would have offered, if she had only had the opportunity: "She would have said sweet little things to me and told me that I was wanted, that I was good for her, and that she loved me."

Much later she and her mother are blissfully reconnected. Elaine reaches out and mother grabs her tiny finger. Cradled in her mother's arms she knows there is someone who understands that she has needs *"right now,"* something not available in the hospital nursery. She takes delight in getting attention from her mother by "cooing and making her smile," rather than by screaming. "I try to speak mostly through my eyes," she says.

## In the Delivery Room

All of a sudden I land in the doctor's hands and he hands me to a nurse, who puts me on the scales. It was cold and I didn't like it. I wanted to lie with my mom, and I'm over on the darn scales! . . .

They stuck me in the heel, to take a blood sample, I think, to see what kind of blood I have.

They are putting something in my eyes and holding me so I won't squirm. Ointment; it's all gummy. I didn't like it because I couldn't open my eyes . . .

Then my footprints. Then my handprints. Then they wrapped me up in a blanket and put me in an incubator.

## If She Had Been in Charge

I would have had the lights down low so it wouldn't have been so bright when I was born.

I would have liked to be put on my mother's stomach; I would have fit there. I didn't know how to fit on the scales.

I would have liked to hear her talk to me. *(Bursts into tears)* I just wanted my mom!

They just wanted me out and over with. It was a routine thing for them . . . I didn't think my mom wanted it that way . . .

## If Her Mom Had Been in Charge

She would have had her legs down. She would have cradled me in her arms next to her side as soon as I was born. My father would have been there supporting her.

She would have said sweet little things to me, told me I was wanted, that I was good for her and that she loved me. I know she was feeling those things, but there was not the opportunity for her to say them directly to me.

## Back with Mother

Mother is sitting up in bed ready to breast-feed me. She looks tired but happy.

I had a blanket, a pink blanket, and I'm trying to look out to see what she looks like. She has her arms out and she's smiling. The nurse is gently handing me to her; I appreciate the gentleness.

My mother cradles me in her left arm and she keeps looking at me and I keep looking at her. I feel like I will reach up and grab her finger. My hand is out of the blanket waving around. She takes it and holds my hand. I feel lots of relief. I feel lots of compassion, and I feel like she is relieved she has me with her. I feel like there is someone who understands that I have needs *right now.*

And I don't want a lot of attention by screaming. I want to get attention by cooing and making her smile. So I try to do those kinds of things, and she responds like crazy. I try to speak mostly through my eyes.

Boy, am I glad that [birth] is over with! I'm glad for the time I'm with my mom.

# *Living with Your Conscious Baby*

*B*abies are not what they used to be. Each new discovery about them inspires further respect and awe. In birth memories, the door stands ajar to the realm of consciousness. It is not the territory of test tubes, weights, and measures but an invisible realm where science walks boldly at one moment and tiptoes shyly the next. As mothers and fathers, touched by the magic of pregnancy, you must wonder how to cope with the unfolding consciousness of your baby.

If birth memories are true, we will have to reassess many of our previous ideas about the nature of babies. Birth reports are charmingly intimate and revealing; they are also revolutionary, confronting us with unimagined intelligence and suggesting that babies deserve a new status, that of conscious persons. They share with the rest of us a capacity for enriched and expanded consciousness, something we are only lately acknowledging in ourselves. Referring to these as "altered states of consciousness," or "unconscious" states, psychology slowly has been introducing us to a range of nonordinary states where things once thought impossible are possible.

In the first American textbook on psychology (1890), Harvard's William James wrote that ordinary waking consciousness was only one type of consciousness, while all around it, "parted by the filmiest of screens," lay potential forms of consciousness entirely different. As examples he listed sleep, dreams, daydreams, hypnotic trances, meditation, and psychic states like telepathy, clairvoyance, and mediumship.

Since the explosion of new interest in mind and consciousness beginning in the 1970s, James's original list has been expanded to include mental states induced by biofeedback, psychedelic drugs, breathing techniques, and near-death experiences. New experiments with deep relaxation, guided fantasy, meditation, and hypnosis have also led to discovery of a diverse bouquet of birth and womb memories, past-life memories, and various forms of extrasensory perception (ESP). The mind of the newborn may embrace all these possibilities.

## Babies in Trance

If you watch, you will see your baby slip into a self-initiated trance at times. Some psychologists call these states "bouts of staring," as infants become completely immobile for 20 to 30 seconds, showing no leg, arm, or eye movements, facial expression, or sound. Eyes are open, but nonconvergent. Episodes usually end with a blink. These trances are what would be called self-hypnosis in adults, and they appear to serve similar purposes: rest, escape from pain or boredom, deep reflection on some past experience, or entertainment. Going into a trance may be a smart thing for a baby to do. Like dreams, those other private altered-state experiences that babies share with us, trances represent creative mental activity and intelligent self-regulation.

## Mind over Brain

A host of new discoveries show that even preborns are intelligently organized long before the brain has had a chance to develop, and that many of your baby's abilities are innate.

Examples are learning, memory, dreaming, expression of personality, and ability to communicate. I think these non-physical, less visible processes are best understood as products of the mind, which follow a different timetable than the brain and can react apart from it. In some surgical near-death experiences, for example, while the brain is anesthetized, the mind is not, and while the brain is strictly limited in location, under certain conditions the mind can "travel" elsewhere and bring back information to prove it.

Belief that brain and mind are separate has been growing slowly in neuroscience since the work of Nobel laureate Sir Charles Sherrington in the 1930s. Though the idea is still not widely accepted, the evidence from studies of out-of-body experience, past-life memory, and other altered states of consciousness make the idea more compelling. It may help you as a parent to think of the brain as a biocomputer used by the mind for all physical activity. This is why brain health or brain damage is so serious. The mind may be working, but a compromised brain prevents normal expression. In my view, it is safe to assume that your baby's mind is working well even while the brain is struggling to mature.

## Mind over Language

You will communicate more easily with your baby if you can set aside the myth that language is the foundation for thought. We are only beginning to understand that thought and communication are more fundamental than language. In fact, some would argue that thinking and communication are innately human, an integral part of consciousness, regardless of age.

As you can observe, your newborn will immediately demonstrate, without any practice, mastery of several universal "languages." Intelligent communication is seen in a range of meaningful cries and sounds, impressive facial expressions, body movement, and hand signals, clear broadcasts of emotion, and in instant imitation of adult gestures and facial expressions.

Until recently, newborns were not given credit for thinking, but thinking is fundamental to learning and to the precise-listening and perceptive-looking activities in which babies engage. None of these activities of the mind wait for development of conventional language. This means that you are not limited to formal language in communicating with your baby.

## Mind over Space

In the past twenty years, extensive study of out-of-body experience (OBE) has resulted in thousands of cases published. Many reports of out-of-body experience come from persons who have experienced death. Survivors of cardiac arrest, violent accidents, or surgical crises, who were clinically dead for a period of time, tell us what it was like to move between life and death. What they discovered will help you appreciate another dimension of your baby's consciousness.

Birth memories often include reports of perceiving oneself and events from a distance, from a perspective above or to the side of the subject's physical location. The baby may find this puzzling. For example:

### *David*

At times I feel like I'm somewhere in the room witnessing what is going on, and at other times I am the child and seeing it from that point of view . . . I wonder how come I can see around behind him?

### Lynn

It's like standing there in the same room. Sometimes I can feel it, and sometimes I'm watching.

### Vicki

It's like flashing back and forth. It's like I am somebody else looking at what's happening. Am I making this up? I don't think I am, but I hesitate to say what I'm actually seeing.

### Laura

I feel weightless, floating. Nobody knows I'm there; they can't even see me. I keep looking through the nursery window; it's weird. I can't be on both sides of the window! I'm looking at the baby; it's me.

Scientist John Lilly writes of his out-of-body experience at the time of birth. He felt he was squeezed, trapped, and dying. He "split off . . . moved out briefly and watched from the outside," where he saw his mother struggling to give birth. For several hours he waited and watched as his head was stuck in the birth canal. Suddenly, he says, the head broke through, the baby came out, and he moved back into the baby's body. He says he left his body many times after birth, usually to go "exploring."

Mind over space is something babies share with adults. Cardiologist Michael Sabom reports several cases in which people have given detailed accounts of their own surgery seen from a vantage point above the operating table. These patients, who knew nothing about surgery, were fully anesthetized and draped and could not have *seen* the operation even if they had been awake. Dr. Sabom put the reports of the respective surgeons and patients side by side for comparison—as I did in my research with mother and child birth memories (chapter 8). They matched.

## Mind over Time

It is disconcerting, but babies know more at birth than they could possibly have learned in nine months inside the womb. When and where could they have learned so much? Their mental activity seems to extend beyond the usual boundaries of time.

A possible answer comes from spectacular cases of past-life memory. Scientific research in this controversial area has advanced greatly in the last few decades, giving us new answers to age-old questions about the mind. We are especially indebted to the scientific work of Ian Stevenson, professor of psychiatry at the University of Virginia Medical School, who has investigated two thousand cases from ten cultures around the world. The results, published in six scholarly volumes to date, are stunning.

Stevenson has been particularly interested in the memories of children, since he believes their earliest memories are less subject to cultural contamination. In 1983 he reported a study of 345 children in India and the United States who claimed to recall a previous lifetime. In the majority of cases he found supportive evidence, including the record of an actual person whose life corresponded with the child's memory.

In both countries children started referring to their past-life memories as soon as they could talk, about age three. Generally they stopped talking about these memories by age five, which is the same time children usually stop talking about their *birth* memories. Some children remembered fifty or more details including numerous proper names, many of which have been verified. In contrast to cases in India, American cases often occurred in families whose members did not believe in reincarnation, and where parents derided, scolded, and occasionally even punished the child for claiming to remember a past life.

Past-life memories were not just an abstraction for these children. Sometimes they insisted on dressing according to the sex they remembered being in their last life. Those who remembered violent death tended to fear the particular instrument or mode of death. They were living their past-life memories, just as people live their birth memories or their out-of-body memories.

Brad, Neville, and Sarah are three of my clients who have displayed feats of mind over time. Brad, age eleven, surprised me with this brief report when asked to go back to the time of his delivery.

### Brad

I can't. I'm out, but it's dark. I'm dead.

I'm dead. All these people around me were crying. I'm not breathing . . .

Now they are putting me down into the ground. I'm in a box, a black box . . . It is 1840. The West. There are cowboys there . . .

Baby Neville was troubled by flashbacks of drowning at his birth. These were apparently related to the method of death in his previous life.

### Neville

It felt like these waters were over my head. I didn't enjoy being in the womb. I felt seasick and sloshed around . . . a drowning feeling. I can't keep my head up above the sloshing water . . .

I see in my mind this wall, a castle or fortress wall, and I see myself falling into the sea, drowning. I was up on this wall . . . a grown man, about thirty . . . depressed, troubled . . .

[At birth again] I am gasping for air . . .

Near the time of her birth, Sarah was upset to find that she was treated like a baby and that her parents did not recognize who she really was. Her memories of a past life as royalty intruded upon her present life. Arrangements were not to her liking.

### Sarah

I'm *not* a baby. I'm old. I'm not any age . . . I've known them. I don't understand why they keep acting like they have just known me for this short time. I'm really frustrated. I am *not* supposed to be the baby; I'm supposed to be in charge.

I know they named me Sarah because Sarah means princess. They *knew* who I was, that's how come they named me Sarah. I wish they would remember, because the more they treat me this way, the harder it is for me to remember who I am. I just don't want them to be in charge, and I can't seem to explain that to them . . . They don't understand.

I'm sitting on the couch . . . looking at my mother and thinking, How did we come to this? *(Laughing)* How come we're in this little house in Pacific Beach on this old couch?

Everyone thinks I'm so precocious . . . I think it's funny. I still have a sense of humor . . . It's so crazy in the world.

## Mind and Self

As you look into the eyes of your baby, you will feel the powerful presence of a person that science has been slow to acknowledge. You yourself may be shy about accepting the signs of decisiveness, judgment, nobility, compassion, and courage found in birth memories. I see them as personal trademarks, fingerprints of self.

Babies show self-consciousness at birth by recognizing and reacting to recordings of their own cries. They show empathy in the way they respond to the cries of their peers and by paying close attention to your difficulties during labor. Babies talk about wanting to reach out and comfort their mothers.

Our inability to grant selfhood to infants may be holding them back from developing their full potential. Linda, whom you met in chapter 8, remarked at sixteen, after recalling her birth, that when she was born she felt "wise" and knew a lot. By the time she was three, however, she had become a conventional child fitting into the role expected of her. She said she became "that dumb little kid" everybody thought she should be and had to grow up and become wise again!

Linda is not alone in expressing her selfhood, of course. Another baby, Marybeth, puts it profoundly: "I felt warm, safe, content, a self-assured child, but very wise, a wise person in a child's body."

Birth memories indicate that babies have an identity of their own; their parents don't give it to them. They act mindfully and build experience around a central core of self. This identity, however, is fragile and subject to challenge. Rejection, constant criticism, or physical abuse can jar that identity, confuse and perhaps even splinter it, leading to problems that will need to be dealt with in psychotherapy years later. But this warping of the self need not take place. With kindness and respect for who they are, you can do more for your children than you ever thought possible.

Like the spectrum of colors that radiate from a prism in sunlight, birth memories reveal the many-splendored dimensions of consciousness.

Birth memories tell you that your baby has a mind. The person using this mind is more ready to communicate with you than you might have guessed. I have a feeling that babies are going to surprise us much more in the future than they have in the past, partly because they have our attention at last. We must be prepared for farfetched stories about newborns saying words, singing simple folk tunes, smiling, or laughing. Babies are more capable than expected. They come bathed in mystery, genius wrapped in swaddling clothes, wearing their baby disguises.

Some of you will find the idea that babies are this conscious unbelievable.

Others will say, "I knew it all the time!"

# A Note about Abortion

*A*bortion is a painful subject to almost everyone. I know some nurses and doctors who have decided not to perform any more abortions, and others who continue to perform them not because they like to but because they earnestly believe it should be an option.

To many who love unborn babies, opposition to abortion is a passionate concern. I share this concern, but I also sympathize with families, particularly women, who have always carried a disproportionate burden for the things that go wrong sexually. I think they must have authority to decide what happens inside their own bodies.

Some of my colleagues have reduced the abortion issue to simple principles that allow them to be all for it or all against it. I have not succeeded in doing that. Abortion issues are unavoidably complex because they involve (1) the integration of science and theology, (2) ethics and politics, (3) moral choices that deal with the welfare of two or more parties, not just one, (4) agonizing psychological decisions, (5) the practice of medicine, (6) civil rights surrounding privacy and matters of conscience, and (6) population problems with global consequences. Underlying all these are issues of a spiritual nature that are matters of personal belief not necessarily shared by others.

My own experiences with birth memory have shown me that human consciousness is more than physical and has continuity and maturity at all ages. I find intelligent life before birth entirely real, though distinctly spiritual in nature. The most accurate description I know for life that is nonphysical but conscious is "spirit." The spirit we are dealing with in early gestational life is a spirit for whom a body is under construction but not yet ready to work.

Spirits without bodies create havoc in legal and legislative areas. This is one of the reasons it is so hard to resolve abortion issues. For practical reasons, spirits need to be fully embodied in order to be treated as persons in our system of jurisprudence. In this light, I think the U.S. Supreme Court was wise in citing physical viability as a prerequisite in contemplating the rights of the unborn.

Who can realistically govern spirits? It is not a task for either church or state, or for science. Personally, I feel secure that the Creator has made proper provision for spirits; I do not believe, as many do, that spirits can be killed by people. The idea that people can "murder" spirits seems theologically presumptuous. With good reason, the life and death of spirits seems to have been put beyond our reach.

When parents contemplate abortion, I assume that the unborn are aware of these thoughts and would be helped to face their circumstance by honest and compassionate communication. Guidelines for this difficult dialogue have been developed by perinatal psychologists (see "Sources and Readings" for details). Following such earnest communication, mothers report they are able to feel love coming from the unborn, experience healing, and feel supported in their decision.

Some feel they must protect the unborn because the unborn cannot protect themselves. This presumption about the spiritual world may not be entirely justified. In my understanding, a spirit is far from helpless. If conditions are not right, a spirit can leave unfinished physical structures behind. Such miscarriages take place frequently for natural reasons, but there may also be room for choice by the unborn. If you were a spirit, would you wait around for an abortion that was already decided and imminent?

In making their own decisions of conscience about abortion, women deserve proper medical care. Abortions poorly done represent a threat to life and health. Back-alley abortions—sought by desperate women for centuries—are still killing people today. In Latin America and Africa, it is estimated that half of all maternal deaths associated with pregnancy arise from illicit abortions. In the Third World, this means a quarter of a million deaths. Not too long ago, this was happening in the United States. Depriving women of medical care is not the way to help babies.

Abortion clinics also give us little to cheer about. They are not happy places for staff, for patients, or for the spirits of the unborn. The business conducted there is solemn business, correcting errors of ignorance, judgment, abuse, and disease. Closing abortion clinics will not end these problems.

In an effort to bring more babies under the protection of the court, some activists seek to lower the recognized age of viability, the age at which premature babies can be saved by heroic medical intervention. This presses medicine into a role it already plays awkwardly—keeping people alive by machines. Because the equipment is available, we are attaching a swelling host of very premature babies to painful, miniaturized life-support equipment in surrealistic nurseries.

Pitiful babies the size of a shoe, their bodies half-constructed, are rushed into these man-made wombs and "miraculously" saved, but at a tragic price—care costing a thousand dollars a day, multiple surgeries, and, for a substantial number, a life of severe handicap. When the Supreme Court set viability at about twenty-eight weeks gestation, it chose a precarious boundary. Now some babies can be saved at twenty-four weeks, but the conditions for achieving this are alarming. Lowering the viability limits would mean unspeakable suffering as more and more poorly embodied babies would end up on machines.

Babies sometimes survive ineffective abortion attempts by their mothers. This life-threatening event registers in the baby's consciousness and, though deeply repressed, can

eventually surface. Until it does, the influence can be insidi-
ous and difficult to resolve because the true problem is not
identified. To the unborn baby, the abortion attempt is
frightening and may create an underlying pattern of distrust,
anger, guilt, or depression that affects behavior for years. A
mother who recognizes the damage the abortion attempt has
inflicted, however, can aid psychological healing through
honest dialog with her child, if she has the courage to do so.

Psychotherapists regularly hear the complaints of clients
who survived their mother's attempt at abortion only to
suffer a fate potentially worse—being unwanted and un-
loved. This condition can inspire a host of miseries, but it is
preventable. Planned parenthood is a practical alternative
helping to assure that every child is wanted, every child
loved. Adoption achieves the same end and should be made
easier.

In the future, medical technology will probably be successful in achieving means of birth control that are truly safe
for both men and women; in this case, abortion will be
greatly reduced. But technology cannot prevent all human
mistakes. People engage in sexual intercourse and then seem
surprised by pregnancy. The solution to abortion lies with
educators as well as doctors. What is needed is a vision of
conscious parenthood, one that distinguishes between making love and making babies, one that affirms life, prepares
for life, and welcomes life.

If everything were perfect, there would be no unwanted
pregnancies and no need for abortion. But as long as there
are imperfections, I believe the evidence given by babies in
remembering their births shows that we should deal with
them as humanely and compassionately as possible.

APPENDIX II

# *A Note about Parental Guilt*

When parents hear that babies remember birth, they are faced with a startling new possibility: that their child had feelings and cognitive faculties right from the beginning and might have been affected in a negative way by what was said and done at birth.

You can't help wondering, What did the baby think? Have I done permanent harm? You may sense a connection between something that happened during pregnancy and how the child has acted since. Perhaps something happened at birth to explain why the child is more or less attached to you. Thoughts like this can stir up guilt.

Here are some things you might do to deal with this kind of guilt:

**Think and Talk about Birth.** It is wise to reflect upon your life during pregnancy, the emotions you had at your child's birth, and any special words that were directed to the baby. The past cannot be reclaimed, but understanding can be a powerful force for healing your guilt. Talking over any mistakes or traumas can benefit both you and your baby.

I think babies have mysterious ways of understanding us when we speak the truth seriously and sincerely. Children wonder and guess about things just as adults do, so their parents' talk about reality brings relief.

You are probably shy about revealing the personal aspects of pregnancy and birth, but these private truths are living history to your child. Such information is rarely available from other sources. You may think you are talking about negative things, but the honest revelation of your inner life is an alchemy that can turn negative feelings into positive ones.

**Stop Practicing Guilt.** You may have gotten into the habit of feeling guilty. Excessive guilt may be a tradition in your family, passed down from grandparents and parents to children. Ask yourself if guilt is your way of showing love. If it is, put on the brakes; concentrate on real ways of expressing love instead.

**Settle for Influence.** A major source of guilt is the belief that being a parent means being in control of everybody and everything in your child's life, which is not really true. When children do something wrong, distraught parents take the blame and wonder what *they* have done wrong. The answer to that question is probably "nothing." You are only one of many forces converging on the life of your child. If you can think of your contribution as influence, not control, your total store of guilt will shrink to proper size.

**Children React Differently.** It should cheer you up to be reminded that children have feelings and thoughts of their own. Look at families with two children who have been treated to the same good (or bad) parents. One becomes a public hero and the other a public embarrassment. It is not the parents' fault but the child's choice that makes the difference.

Kids can fool you by not caring about things you assumed were important. All children do not react in the same way to a trauma. I think this is because some are more advanced than others. A mother in my study felt guilty for a spontaneous remark made in the delivery room. She had said—half in jest, half in truth—"What an ugly looking monster!" But the comment did not show up in the daughter's birth memory. Perhaps it didn't "stick" in her mind, or she was mature enough to discount it. According to both mother and daughter, their relationship was a good one.

**Learning from Babies.**   Parents aren't perfect, but trying to be a good one means acknowledging errors. One mother's remark to the doctor, "Why didn't you just wrap the cord around her neck and strangle her," caused a rift between mother and child that lasted many years. These two needed to talk, to neutralize that poison and find common ground. In such cases, guilt can best serve by focusing on reconciliation, on *learning* rather than regret.

We have been slow to accept the role of babies as teachers. They take you—unready, not knowing what to do—and make you into a parent. You make mistakes, it's true, but they keep letting you know what they need. Babies know when they are hungry, for example, and teach you this better than you can teach them. Your need to learn may be your best asset. As your baby grows, you learn more and more.

Can you relate to a mere babe displaying wisdom and courage? Be on the lookout for subtle gestures of comfort and love directed your way. Your baby watches over you, takes note of your happiness or discouragement, tries to distract or entertain you, and may even start a filibuster when a third party is causing trouble.

Perhaps, along with other things, your baby knows your guilt and is trying to help you with it. Can you open yourself to this possibility?

# Sources and Readings

## Introduction: The Truth about Newborns

One of the first to focus international attention on what birth was like from the baby's point of view was the French obstetrician Frederick Leboyer (1975), *Birth Without Violence,* New York: Alfred Knopf.

For the most comprehensive review of all aspects of infant pain, see K. J. S. Anand and P. R. Hickey (1987), "Pain and Its Effects in the Human Neonate and Fetus," *New England Journal of Medicine* 317, 1,321–1,329.

Among the few books celebrating the wide-ranging abilities of newborns are: Tom Bower (1977), *A Primer of Infant Development,* San Francisco: W. H. Freeman; Edward Tronick and Lauren Adamson (1980), *Babies As People: New Findings on Our Social Beginnings,* New York: Collier Books; Marshall Klaus and Phyllis Klaus (1985), *The Amazing Newborn,* Reading, Mass.: Addison-Wesley. The view of noted Swiss psychologist Jean Piaget (which, in my opinion, does a disservice to newborns) was stated by Burton White in 1975 and again in the 1985 revised edition of his book, *The First Three Years of Life,* New York: Prentice Hall Press, pp. 12–30.

The first textbook in the new field of pre- and perinatal psychology is Thomas Verny, ed. (1987), *Pre & Perinatal Psychology: An Introduction,* New York: Human Sciences Press.

In North America, the organization focusing attention on all aspects of birth psychology is the Pre & Perinatal Psychology Association of North America (PPPANA), founded by Dr. Thomas Verny in 1983 and open to all interested persons. The association has held biennial international congresses in Toronto (1983), San Diego (1985), and San Francisco (1987). Members receive the *Pre & Perinatal Psychology Journal* and a periodic newsletter.

For information, write to PPPANA Headquarters, 13 Summit Terrace, Dobbs Ferry, N.Y. 10522.

In Europe, the organization dealing with issues of prenatal psychology is the International Society for Study of Prenatal Psychology and Medicine (ISPP), founded in 1971. The ISPP has held eight congresses and symposia. For information about their triennial conferences (now including English translations), write to the president, Dr. Peter Fedor-Freybergh, at Engelbrektsgatan 19, S-114, 32, Stockholm, Sweden.

If you think you need some form of birth therapy, the following resources may be helpful. Professional hypnotherapists may be sought through the American Society of Clinical Hypnosis, Des Plaines, Ill. (312-297-3317) or the American Academy of Medical Hypnoanalysis, 1-800-34HYPNO, with headquarters in Akron, Ohio. Members include physicians and psychologists. To locate lay workers with a spiritual approach to birth problems, call Rebirth International at 1-800-641-4545, Ext. 232. One of the few places offering a range of intensive birth-therapy options is The Pocket Ranch in Healdsburg, Calif. (707-431-1516).

## Chapter 1. Growing a Body and Brain

There are different ways of estimating the age of the fetus. Some prefer "menstrual age" or crown-rump length, the measure of the fetus from crown to rump; in this system forty weeks is full term. Embryologists are interested in age from the day of fertilization, so they count in days and weeks; in this system thirty-eight weeks is full term.

The most famous intrauterine photographs of conception and development in the womb are those of Lennart Nilsson (1977), *A Child Is Born,* rev. ed., New York: Delacorte; and the Nilsson film (1983) *The Miracle of Life,* Boston: WBGH Educational Foundation.

Parents will find inspiration in embryology according to Geraldine Flanagan (1965), *The First Nine Months of Life,* New York and Toronto: Life Cycle Books. The technical and definitive studies of the fetus at the University of Pittsburgh began with Davenport Hooker (1952), *The Prenatal Origin of Behavior,* Lawrence, Kans.: Univ. of Kansas Press.

Prenatal exercise patterns are revealed by L. G. R. Van Dongen and E. G. Goudie (1980), "Fetal Movement Patterns in the First Trimester of Pregnancy," *British Journal of Obstetrics & Gynecology* 87, 191–193; and by A. William Liley (1972), "The Foetus as a Personality," *Australian & New Zealand Journal of Psychiatry* 6 (2), 99–105.

A parent's guide to dealing with teratogens is Ronald and Barbara Gots (1977), *Caring for Your Unborn Child,* New York: Stein & Day. The danger of abnormalities associated with alcohol consumption around the time of conception is revealed by Claire Ernhart, R. Sokol, and others (1987), "Alcohol Teratogenicity in the Human: A Detailed Assessment of Specificity, Critical Period, and Threshold," *American Journal of Obstetrics & Gynecology* 156 (1), 33–39.

Leading the movement to understand the fluid brain are Richard Bergland (1985), *The Fabric of Mind,* New York: Viking; and Candace Pert (1987), "Neuropeptides: The Emotions and Bodymind," *Noetic Sciences Review* 2 (Spring), 13–18.

## Chapter 2. Alert and Aware

Those seeking detailed documentation of the newborn senses will find 200 references in David B. Chamberlain (1983), *Consciousness at Birth: A Review of the Empirical Evidence,* available from Chamberlain Communications, 909 Hayes Ave., San Diego, Calif. 92103 ($8.00, including sales tax and postage). For the latest technical review of infant senses and perception, see Phillip Salapatek and Leslie Cohen, eds. (1987), *Handbook of Infant Perception,* Vol. 1, New York: Academic Press.

For the pioneering work of Henry Truby on the infant cry, see John Lind, ed. (1965), "The Newborn Infant Cry," *Acta Paediatrica Scandinavica* 163 (Supplement). A recent review of all cry studies is Barry M. Lester and C. F. Z. Boukydis, eds. (1985), *Infant Crying,* New York: Plenum.

## Chapter 3. Learning and Remembering

Interesting information on life before birth, including the prenatal memories of Boris Brott, are found in Thomas Verny and John Kelley (1981), *The Secret Life of the Unborn Child,* New York: Summit Books.

All aspects of newborn cognition are reviewed with 250 citations in David B. Chamberlain (1987), "The Cognitive Newborn: A Scientific Update," *British Journal of Psychotherapy* 4 (1), 30–71.

Infant recognition of voices is featured in studies by Jacques Mehler, Josiane Bertoncini, and others (1978), "Infant Recognition of Mother's Voice," *Perception* 7, 491–497; and by Anthony De-Casper and William Fifer (1980), "Of Human Bonding: Newborns Prefer Their Mothers' Voices," *Science* 208, 1,174–1,176.

Breakthrough studies of the infant's ability to imitate were made by Andrew Meltzoff and Keith Moore (1977), "Imitation of Facial and Manual Gestures by Human Neonates," *Science* 198, 75–78; and by Tiffany M. Field and others (1982), "Discrimination and Imitation of Facial Expressions by Neonates," *Science* 218, 179–181.

The special advantages of early contact of newborns with parents are reviewed by Marshall Klaus and John Kennell (1983), "Early Events: Later Effects on the Infant," in *Frontiers of Infant Psychiatry,* Justin Call, Eleanor Galenson, and Robert Tyson, eds., New York: Basic Books, 7–16.

Publications and workshops are offered in many cities by the Infant Stimulation Education Association, UCLA Center for Health Sciences, Factor Building 5-942, Los Angeles, Calif. 90024; and by The Better Baby Institute, 8801 Stenton Ave., Philadelphia, Pa. 19118.

For books, manuals, and tapes on communicating with your unborn child, see Evlyn Bowen (1988), *Lovestart,* Los Angeles: Hay House; and The Prenatal University, 27225 Calaroga, Hayward, Calif. 94545.

A sympathetic overview of infant learning and memory processes is provided by Carolyn Rovee-Collier and Lewis P. Lipsitt (1982), "Learning, Adaptation, and Memory," in *Psychobiology of the Human Newborn,* Paul Stratton, ed., London and New York: Wiley & Sons, chapter 7.

## Chapter 4. The Engaging Personality

Sir William Liley (1972) was one of the first to focus on the personality of the fetus in a fascinating paper, "The Foetus as a Personality," *Australian & New Zealand Journal of Psychiatry* 6 (2), 99–105.

The dream life of newborns, including premature babies, was decisively charted by Howard P. Roffwarg, Joseph Muzio, and William Dement (1966), "Ontogenetic Development of the Human Sleep-Dream Cycle," *Science* 152, 604–619.

T. G. R. Bower appreciates the meaning of infant smiles in chapters 3 and 7 of *A Primer of Infant Development*, San Francisco: W. H. Freeman.

The revealing film of a father and baby communicating in synchrony was taken by Daniel N. Stern and reported by Louis W. Sander (1980) in "New Knowledge about the Infant from Current Research: Implications for Psychoanalysis," *Journal of the American Psychoanalytic Association* 28, 181–198.

Much information about infants, including the story of the masked feeding experiment, is found in Edward Tronick and Lauren Adamson (1980), *Babies as People: New Findings on Our Social Beginnings*, New York: Collier Books.

## Chapter 5. A Gifted Communicator

A photo of a fetus who looks totally entranced while holding the umbilical cord is found in Lennart Nilsson (1976), *A Child Is Born*, rev. ed., New York: Delacorte Press, p. 118.

World literature on squalling in the womb is comprehensively reviewed by George H. Ryder (1943), "Vagitus Uterinus," *American Journal of Obstetrics & Gynecology* 46, 867–872. The many meanings of cry sounds after birth are reviewed by Barry M. Lester and C. F. Z. Boukydis, eds. (1985), *Infant Crying*, New York: Plenum.

Infant hand signals were noted by Hanus and Mechtilde Papousek (1977), "Mothering and the Cognitive Head-Start: Psychobiological Considerations," in *Studies in Mother-Infant Interaction*, ed. H. R. Schaffer, London: Academic Press, 70–71.

Pioneering studies of infant communication are described in T. Berry Brazelton and Heidelise Als (1979), "Four Early Stages in the Development of Mother-Infant Interaction," *The Psychoanalytic Study of the Child* 34, 349–369; Heidelise Als (1977), "The Newborn Communicates," *Journal of Communication* 27, 66–73; and Colwyn Trevarthen (1980), "The Foundations of Intersubjectivity: Development of Interpersonal and Cooperative Understanding in Infants," in *The Social Foundations of Language and Thought: Essays in Honor of Jerome S. Bruner,* ed. David R. Olson, New York: W. W. Norton, chapter 14.

Infant superiority in hearing the smallest segments of speech sound was discovered by Janet F. Werker and Richard C. Tees (1984), "Cross-Language Speech Perception: Evidence for Perceptual Reorganization During the First Year of Life," *Infant Behavior & Development* 7, 49–63. Infant skill in lip reading was shown by Barbara Dodd (1979), "Lip Reading in Infancy: Attention to Speech Presented In- and Out-of-Synchrony," *Cognitive Psychology* 11, 478–484.

M. Scaife and Jerome Bruner (1975) proved "The Capacity for Joint Visual Attention in the Infant," *Nature* 253, 265–256.

## Chapter 6. Discovering Birth Memory

Records of birth memory obtained in hypnosis span the century, from a book in French by Albert de Rochas citing experiments in the 1890s, to the article by David B. Chamberlain (1988), "The Significance of Birth Memories," *Pre & Perinatal Psychology Journal* 2 (Summer), 136–154. Significant advances have been made in this field by Leslie M. LeCron (1954), "A Hypnotic Technique for Uncovering Unconscious Material," *International Journal of Clinical and Experimental Hypnosis,* vol. 2, 1–3, and vol. 11, 137–142; and by David B. Cheek (1975), "Maladjustment Patterns Apparently Related to Imprinting at Birth," *American Journal of Clinical Hypnosis* 18 (2), 75–82.

The first leader in developing a psychology of birth, beginning around 1904, was Otto Rank, author of *The Trauma of Birth* (New York: Brunner, 1952). He has been followed by other pioneers, including Nandor Fodor (1949), *The Search for the Beloved: A Clinical Investigation of the Trauma of Birth and Prenatal Condition,* New York: Hermitage; L. Ron Hubbard (1950), *Dianetics,* Los Angeles: Scientology Publications; Arthur Janov (1970), *The Primal Scream,* New York: Putnam; and Stanislav Grof (1975), *Realms of the Human Unconscious,* New York: Viking.

The latest books about the theory and method of rebirthing are by Sondra Ray (1985), *Ideal Birth,* and Sondra Ray and Bob Mandel (1987), *Birth and Relationships: How Your Birth Affects Your Relationships,* both published by Celestial Arts, Berkeley, Calif.

Educational videotapes for parents in the area of prenatal and birth psychology are: "A Gift for the Unborn Child," Bradley Boatman Productions, Malibu, Calif., distributed by Ferde Grofe Films, 3100 Airport Ave., Santa Monica, Calif. 90405; and "Knowing the Unborn," Pre-Birth Parenting, 2554 Lincoln Blvd., #509, Marina del Rey, Calif. 90291.

## Chapter 7. Little Children Remember

I invite readers to send me copies of birth memories reported by very young children. Send them to Chamberlain Communications, 909 Hayes Ave., San Diego, Calif. 92103.

Linda Mathison of Seattle was the first to gather information about the birth memories of two- and three-year-old children. I am grateful to Linda and to *Mothering* magazine for permission to use some of her stories. Linda A. Mathison (1981), "Does Your Child Remember?" *Mothering,* Fall, 103–107.

The charming story of the two-year-old in a tub is contributed by psychiatrist Rima Laibow (1986), "Birth Recall: A Clinical Report," *Pre & Perinatal Psychology Journal* 1 (Fall), 78–81. Anthropologist Robbie Davis-Floyd relates the first-person account of her child who reported "snake" and "doggie" companions in the womb.

For the story of the secret revealed by a three-year-old, I am indebted to Cathy Morales and the editors of *NAPSAC News,* where the story appeared in the Spring issue of 1983.

## Chapter 8. Memories That Match

For the full story about matching memories, see David B. Chamberlain (1986) "Reliability of Birth Memories: Evidence from Mother and Child Pairs in Hypnosis," *Journal of the American Academy of Medical Hypnoanalysts* 1 (December), 89–98. This research was originally presented to the American Society of Clinical Hypnosis, Minneapolis, November 1980. Information about the availability of all of the author's scholarly papers may be obtained from Chamberlain Communications, 909 Hayes Ave., San Diego, Calif. 92103. Please include a self-addressed, stamped envelope.

Key research on the reliability and validity of birth memory in hypnosis has been done by David B. Cheek (1974), "Sequential Head and Shoulder Movements Appearing with Age Regression in Hypnosis to Birth," *American Journal of Clinical Hypnosis* 16 (4), 261–266 (see also David Cheek and Ernest Rossi [1988], *Mind-Body Therapy*, New York: W. W. Norton); Vladimir L. Raikov (1980), "Age Regression to Infancy by Adult Subjects in Deep Hypnosis," *American Journal of Clinical Hypnosis* 22 (3), 156–163; and Vladimir Raikov (1982), "Hypnotic Age Regression to the Neonatal Period: Comparisons with Role Playing," *International Journal of Clinical & Experimental Hypnosis* 30 (2), 108–116.

For advanced discussion of hypnosis and memory, see Helen M. Pettinati, ed. (1988), *Hypnosis and Memory*, New York: Guilford Press. The mechanisms of memory on a cellular level are reviewed by Arnold Buchheimer (1987), "Memory: Preverbal and Verbal," in *Pre and Perinatal Psychology: An Introduction*, Thomas Verny, ed., New York: Human Sciences Press, 55–62.

## Conclusion: Living with Your Conscious Baby

John Lilly (1978) reports on his out-of-body experience at birth in *The Scientist: A Novel Autobiography*, Philadelphia: J. P. Lippincott. For a convenient summary of the research on out-of-body experience, see chapter 12 in Kenneth Ring (1981), *Life at Death: A Scientific Investigation of the Near-Death Experience*, New York: Coward, McCann, & Geoghegan. The separation of mind and body during emergency surgery is dramatically illustrated in chapter 6 of Michael B. Sabom (1982), *Recollections of Death: A Medical Investigation*, New York: Wallaby Books/Simon and Schuster.

Rare information on the altered states of newborns is found in T. Berry Brazelton (1962), "Observations of the Neonate," *Journal of the American Academy of Child Psychiatry* 1, 55–56; Brian Hopkins and Titia V. W. Palthe, "Staring in Infancy," *Early Human Development* 12, 261–267; and David B. Cheek (1986), "Prenatal and Perinatal Imprints: Apparent Prenatal Consciousness as Revealed by Hypnosis," *Pre & Perinatal Psychology Journal* 1 (Winter) 97–110.

The rigorous work of medical professor Ian Stevenson—a milestone in our understanding of mind and memory—is published in six volumes by the University Press of Virginia. The latest is *Cases of the Reincarnation Type* (1979). His work on the past-life memories of children (1984) is "American Children Who Claim to Remember Previous Lives," *Journal of Nervous and Mental Disease* 171, 742–748.

## *Appendix I. A Note about Abortion*

The beginnings of a system for communicating with the unborn are described by Helen Watkins (1986), "Treating the Traumas of Abortion," *Pre & Perinatal Psychology Journal* 1 (2), 135–142; and Clara M. Riley (1987), "Transuterine Communication in Problem Pregnancies," *Pre & Perinatal Psychology Journal* 1 (3), 180–190. Tapes (in a choice of four languages) are available on "Mother/Fetus Communication" from Clara Riley, Ph.D., 31542 Coast Highway, Suite #2, South Laguna, Calif. 92677.

# ABOUT THE AUTHOR

Dr. David Chamberlain is a psychologist, Vice President of the Pre- and Perinatal Association of North America and member of the American Society of Clinical Hypnosis. He received his Ph.D. from Boston University. His groundbreaking work has been praised by Frederick Leboyer, author of *Birth Without Violence*; Dr. Ashley Montagu; renowned childbirth educator Sheila Kitzinger; Thomas Verney, M.D., author of *The Secret Life of the Unborn Child*; LaUna Huffines, author of *Bridge of Light*; and medical and psychological professionals throughout the world.

Thr /. 5/